React

Quickstart Step-By-Step Guide To Learning React Javascript library

Lionel Lopez

© Copyright 2017 by Lionel Lopez - All rights reserved.

If you would like to share this book with another person, please purchase an additional copy for each recipient. Thank you for respecting the hard work of this author. Otherwise, the transmission, duplication or reproduction of any of the following work including specific information will be considered an illegal act irrespective of if it is done electronically or in print. This extends to creating a secondary or tertiary copy of the work or a recorded copy and is only allowed with express written consent from the Publisher. All additional right reserved.

TABLE OF CONTENT

1. **Introducing React**..9

a. Introduction
b. History & Reason Of Popularity:
c. Reason of popularity:
d. What is State Management?

2. **Main principles of React**...................................14

a. Write HTML using JavaScript:
b. You can use the JSX compromise:
c. Reusable, composable components:
d. Virtual views in memory:
e. Views are a function of state:
f. One-way flow of data (and behavior):
g. It's just JavaScript:

3. **Building your first react app**............................17

a. Installation
a.i.1. HTML Node JS
a.i.2. Directory Explanation

4. Components in React..27

- a. Components Introduction
- b. What are components in React?
- c. How to create a component?
- d. Passing values to Components?
- e. Function components:
- f. Composing Components Multiple Times:

5. Styling in React...42

- a. Installing Bootstrap
- b. Radium
- c. Useful option for styling in react

6. Creating complex components.......................................54

- a. Converting theme to React

7. Installing and Using jQuery Plugins in ReactJS............70

- a. Installing SlimScroll

8. Transferring properties...76

- a. Transferring Values
- b. Transferring Functions

9. Dealing with State...87

- a. Difference Between States and Properties

10. Integrating React with Yii 2...99

- a. Installing Yii2
- b. Installing React In Yii2

11. Going from Data to UI 109

12. The component lifecycle 127

- a. Introduction to ReactJS component lifecycle
- b. componentWillMount
- c. componentDidMount
- d. componentWillReceiveProps
- e. shallComponentUpdate
- f. componentWillUpdate
- g. componentDidUpdate
- h. componentWillUnMount

13. Creating a single page app using react router 132

- a. Introduction
- b. Installation
- c. Using Route
- d. Child Route

14. Setting up your react development environment 170

- a. Installing create-react-app Globally
- b. Directory Explanation
- c. Building Application
- d. Serving Application after successful build

15.   Test your React application with Jest 176

- a. Jest Introduction
- b. Getting Started

- **c.** Small Test
- **d.** Testing Components

16. Charge your React application with Redux........183

- **a.** Redux Introduction
- **b.** Redux Three Principles
- **c.** Installing Redux
- **d.** Counter App In Redux React

17. Build and go beyond...199

Chapter 1

Introduction React

Introduction

This book is about React, A book written for React tutorial. React is based on JavaScript. Let me tell you, what is JavaScript? JavaScript is a web based programming language and it was created by Brendan Eich, co-founder of Mozilla project. Along with HTML and CSS, JavaScript is the core of World Wide Web and it is one of the most popular languages of all time.

Versions of JavaScript with release dates:

- **First Version - 1996**
- **Second Version - 1998**
- **Third Version - 1999**
- **Fourth Version - Abandoned due to some issues.**
- **Fifth Version - 2009**
- **5.1 Version - 2011**
- **Sixth Version - 2015**

This book is for those who are looking for react book that teaches ReactJS from beginning to advance level. This teaches you React basic and advanced concepts.

Things you should know before learning ReactJS:

There are couple things you should know before learning ReactJS. Learning React JS requires knowledge of Node JS and JavaScript, Here are more things you should know, before diving into ReactJS:

- Basic Knowledge Of HTMl, CSS and JavaScript
- Important Programming Concepts
- Dom Manipulation

ReactJS is a JavaScript library to create User Interfaces. React was first created by Jordan Walke software engineer on Facebook. React was deployed on Facebook news feed on 2011 and later on 2012, it was deployed on Instagram. It allows developers to create large scale applications. React is currently deployed on NetFlix, Facebook, Instagram, Airbnb, Wallmart, and Imgur. Initially, ReactJS was not open source. In May 2013, it was open sourced. Its main goal is to allow developers to create Web Apps that are fast, simple and scalable. Here are some reasons to choose ReactJS

- One-way data flow.
- Virtual Dom.

- JSX.
- JavaScript Expressions.
- Routing.

React is component based, In React, component can manage their own state to build complex UI, for example If a user is logged in, then show logout link otherwise show login form in same component. React also supports React Native to build native apps in react, we can build IOS and Android apps in React Native that is 100% free. React can easily update view on data changes. React also provides Routing, Routing includes Frontend Routing, in react routing is something is different, Routing is based on components: React can be used to build very large applications, which makes applications very fast and accurate. Here are some reactions about React:

"The most fun UI lib I ever played with :) Compared to other approaches and libs that tackle data binding and DOM events, this one was the easiest to understand and become productive with."

"I am new to ReactJS and I can find ReactJS one of the easiest frameworks. I am a blogger and I have choose react for blogging on my site, using Code Pen I can easy put demos in my site."

React is created by gigantic Facebook. One of most used social networking website. I prefer you to use React for future JavaScript applications because React is supported by gigantic Facebook and other popular contributors.

History & Reason of Popularity:

React was first created by Facebook Software Engineer Jordan Walke, He was inspired by XHP, an HTML component framework for PHP. Initially, React was not open sourced, Facebook implemented React in their news feed in 2011 and on 2013 they Facebook build Instagram on React, and now Instagram is completely built on ReactJS

On 2013, ReactJS was open sourced by Facebook in JavaScript conference. Now ReactJS is one of the most popular frameworks of all time.

Reason of popularity:

The reason of popularity is ReactJS is due to following features

- One-way data flow.
- Virtual DOM.
- JSX.
- JavaScript expressions in view libraries.
- React Native
- Every component must have a method render that returns view.
- Easy to understand
- View gets automatically changed when something changed on input.
- One of most problems of computer programming is state management, React provides practices to handle state management.

What is State Management in React?

React provides states features, States handles data for components, like input that contains a string, Boolean that contains true or false, let's suppose you want to show login form is user is not logged in and show logout button if user is logged in. This can be handled by React JS states. We can easily change view according to state.

It means we can change views of a component according to some state. As defined above clearly.

Chapter 2
Main Principles of React

React JS is only JavaScript in a tuxedo implying that the standards of JavaScript likewise apply to React JS, yet wearing a tuxedo additionally gives you certain benefits in life, similar to individuals approach you with deference and many believe you're flying with every available amenity at an air terminal.

To make the long story short the designers at Facebook realized that JavaScript has an enormous and I mean an immense biological community around it that is the reason there are numerous libraries work around it despite the fact that it's an idiosyncratic dialect. React, Redux and Flux all have diverse standards or thoughts behind them and engineers at Facebook ensured that they can work with React JS

- **Write HTML using JavaScript:**

HTML is extraordinary for static information, yet not all that good for dynamic evolving information. Rather than utilizing a format dialect set up of HTML, ReactJS route is to simply create HTML utilizing the JavaScript dialect itself.

- **You can use the JSX compromise:**

Since we cherish HTML, there is a bargain to motivate us to compose HTML in JavaScript yet at the same time utilize a punctuation like HTML. It the JSX JavaScript expansion.

- **Reusable and Composable Components:**

Much the same as HTML itself, and adding to what HTML effectively offer, with React you characterize little segments and set up them together to shape greater ones. You can reuse parts as you wish crosswise over ventures (and even crosswise over aggregate targets)

- **Virtual views in memory:**

Before controlling the DOM in the program, ReactJS registers the "yield" of an application in memory (which is quick). At the point when refreshes happen, it "diffs" what it has with what is coming and performs just the base required real DOM operations?

- **Views are a function of state:**

You compose that "capacity" once and it'll generally mirror the present state. We don't have to physically perform DOM operations to mirror the new state, ReactJS will do that for us.

- **One-way flow of data (and behavior):**

There is no MVC, you stream the application information through props to any parts that need information. You can likewise stream callbacks for youngster's parts to get to specific activities of the application. Youngster's parts can't straightforwardly read or compose the application state. Composing parts with very much characterized and obliged duties that don't meddle with others is the thing that makes awesome React applications.

- **It's just JavaScript:**

React has a little API which is fundamentally a couple of capacities that you can learn in a couple of hours. From that point onward, your JavaScript abilities are what makes you a decent React engineer.

Chapter 3
Building your first React App

We cannot start working on a JavaScript framework without knowing about installation of framework. In this chapter we will learn following things:

- Installing React in plain HTML.
- Installing React using Node JS.
    - HelloWorld Example in Node JS ReactJS

"NOTE: Remember I will use Node JS CLI in future chapters, because CLI is very important rather than React in plain HTML. Every ReactJS project developers uses Node JS to start React JS projects. So we will focus on learning Node JS based React".

Before getting started with a programming language. It is important to setup its environment, with ReactJS we need to setup ReactJS environment. ReactJS can be installed by two ways:

First Way:

To install react in plain HTML, we need following libraries to include in our web app and Babel as JavaScript preprocessor to process ES6 standard:

React Itself:

https://cdnjs.cloudflare.com/ajax/libs/react/15.3.1/reactjsmin.js

React DOM:

https://cdnjs.cloudflare.com/ajax/libs/react/15.3.1/react-dom.min.js

Babel:

While including these libraries, Our Initial React Application should look like this:

```
<!DOCTYPE html>
<html>
<head>
    <title>React Hello World</title>
</head>
<body>
    <div id="root" ></div>

    <script type="text/javascript" src="react.min.js" ></script>
    <script type="text/javascript" src="react-dom.min.js" ></script>
    <script type="text/javascript" src="browser.min.js" ></script>
    <script type="text/babel">
```

```
            var HellWorld = React.createClass({
                render: function() {
                    return (
                        <div>
                            {this.props.children}
                        </div>
                    );
                }
            });

            var destination = document.querySelector("#root");

            ReactDOM.render(
                <div>
                    <HellWorld>Hello World</HellWorld>
                </div>,
                destination
            );

        </script>
    </body>
</html>
```

If this code works successfully, our screen will be greeted with printed Hello World.

Second Way (CLI):

To install React using cli, we need Node JS to install, You can download NODE JS <u>here</u>, After Node JS installs, go to CMD in windows or terminal in Mac/Ubuntu. Type following command:

```
npm install -g create-react-app
```

This will install create-react-app globally that will help us to create apps easily and anywhere in our computer. Remember if you are a PHP developer, you don't need to put REACT JS applications in server like www folder of Xampp and htdocs of Xampp. When this installation gets complete, we can install react using:

```
create-react-app my-app
cd my-app
npm start
```

This will create my-app directory and will install a complete react app setup. ReactJS app will be available on <u>http://localhost:3000</u>, on new app, a message will be print like this:

Directory Explanation:

After installation of ReactJS CLI application, The ReactJS application folder structure should look like this:

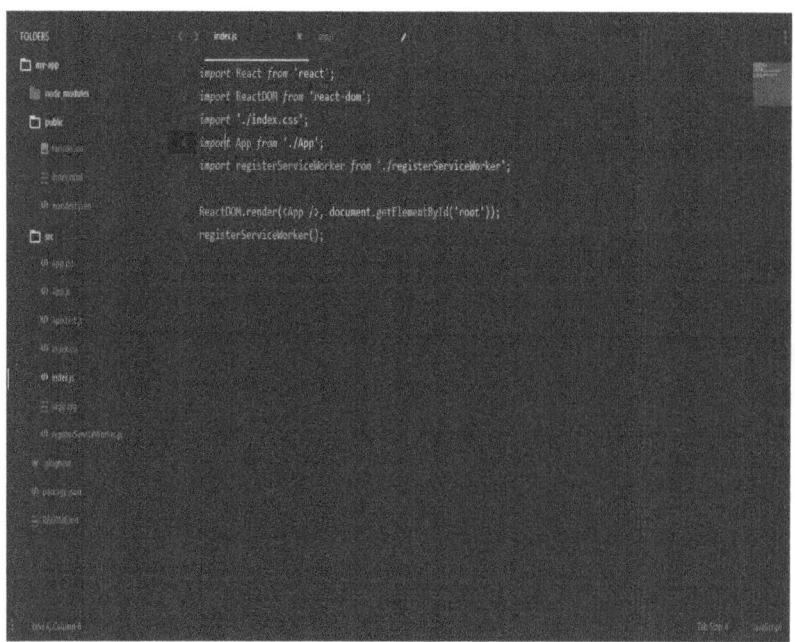

So there are three folders, node_modules, public, src.

node_modules: Node modules contains all important libraries like React, reactDOM, react-router etc.

Public: Public folder contains public assets such as images, icons, files and other important files that can be imported to app.

src: Src stands for source, this folder contains JavaScript source files or react app, Which is built on JavaScript, It mean this folder contains JavaScript files.

Let's create a hello world example in react cli app. Now delete all files in src folder, make it empty. Now create two files in src folder,

- index.js
- HelloWorld.js

src/index.js

import React from 'react';
import ReactDOM from 'react-dom';
import HelloWorld from './HelloWorld.js';

ReactDOM.render(
 <HelloWorld/>,
 document.getElementById('root')

)

src/HelloWorld.js

```
import React from 'react';
import ReactDOM from 'react-dom';

export default class HelloWorld extends React.Component{
    render() {
        return (
            <div>
                <h1>HelloWorld</h1>
            </div>
        );
    }
}
```

This will print hello world on screen.

HelloWorld

So far we have learned about

- React
- Principles of React
- Creating an App in React

In this chapter we have learned how to installed ReactJS and created hello world example. Here is the exercise in the last:

src/HelloWorld.js

```
import React from 'react';
import ReactDOM from 'react-dom';

export default class HelloWorld extends React.Component{
    render() {
        return (
            <div>
                <h1>HelloWorld</h1>
            </div>
        );
    }
}
```

src/index.js

```
import React from 'react';
import ReactDOM from 'react-dom';
import HelloWorld from './HelloWorld.js';


ReactDOM.render(
    <HelloWorld/>,
```

document.getElementById('root')
)

We have ended our chapter and we have learned how to create an application. So here are some questions:

- What is create-react-app?
- What is node_modules folder and why it is used for?

Answers for the questions:

What is create-react-app?

create-react-app is CLI command, this command is provided by ReactJS to install Node JS based ReactJS Application. We can install this command by using:

```
npm install create-react-app –g
```

This will install this cli command globally so we can install by:

```
npm install create-react-app
```

What is node_modules folder and why it is used for?

node_modules folder contains build tools. node_modules folder contains all libraries which are installed using npm install or yarn install. You will another file package.json, which defines libraries that will install.

Chapter 4
Components

So, what are components in programming? Components are building blocks of applications, Components helps us to split large applications into components, to make it easier to modify and understand.

What are components in React?

Components are Heart of React! Every react application has components. You can say ReactJS is based on components. According to ReactJS definition:

"Components allows you to split the UI interface into small, reusable pieces. Components are based on JavaScript functions. They accepts props, parameters or we can say arguments and return React elements describing what should appear on the screen. Components are heart of ReactJS, components build our ReactJS application".

According to book definition, the component allows us to split react app into small pieces, like **Navbar**, **Footer**, **Main Content**, **Cards**, **Images** and etc. Component is building part of application.

One thing more, every component must have a render function that renders a view, For example, a footer component renders footer view and navbar component renders navbar view and so on.

How to create a component?

Do you have ever think how to create components? How they look like? How to use them? How to compose Components multiple times? Let's learn all these things now. Components in react can be created by React.Component keyword. Now create a new HTML file:

Index.html

```
<!DOCTYPE html>
<html>
<head>
        <title>React Hello World</title>
</head>
<body>
        <div id="root" ></div>


        <script type="text/javascript" src="react.min.js" ></script>
        <script type="text/javascript" src="react-dom.min.js" ></script>
```

```
<script type="text/javascript" src="browser.min.js" ></script>
<script type="text/babel">
    var Navbar = React.createClass({
        render: function () {
            return (
                <div className='navbar navbar-default' >
                    <div className="navbar-header" >
                        <a className="navbar-brand" >React</a>
                    </div>
                    <div className="collapse navbar-collapse" >
                        <ul className="navbar-nav nav navbar-right" >
                            <li>
                                <a>Home Page</a>
                            </li>
                        </ul>
                    </div>
                </div>
            );
```

```
        }
    });
    var HellWorld = React.createClass({
        render: function() {
            return (
                <div>
                    <h1>{this.props.children}</h1>
                </div>
            );
        }
    });

    var destination = document.querySelector("#root");

    ReactDOM.render(
        <div>
            <Navbar />
            <HellWorld>Hello World</HellWorld>
        </div>,
        destination
    );

    </script>
</body>
```

</html>

This will print:

React

- Home Page

HelloWorld

Passing values to Components?

Just like parameters we can also pass values to ReactJS components, and in React we call them props, we can pass props by:

<NavBar brandName='React Book' />

Just like attribute. Even we can pass functions as props. We have passed props in NavBar, now we will use **brandName** in Navbar.js, so we can replace this code:

<a className="navbar-brand" >**React**</a>

Into

```
<a className="navbar-brand" >{this.props.brandName}</a>
```

This will print:

React Book

- Home Page

HelloWorld

Functional Based components:

You what does mean by a function, and you can see functional components in heading, you might be worrying what functional components are? In ReactJS, components can be composed by functions, we can pass parameter called props to that functions we can use that props in our components according to our needs.

```
function Welcome(props) {
    return (
        <div>
            <p>Hello World</p>
        </div>
    );
}
```

We can use this component by same as a component that is created by React.Component(). Benefit of using this technique is that we can easily create many components by just making functions, these are called Functional components, just like this:

```
function Welcome(props) {
  return (
    <div>
     <p>Hello World</p>
    </div>
  );
}
<Welcome />

function Button(props) {
  return (
    <button className={this.props.btnClass} >
      {this.props.text}
    </button>
  );
}
<Button text='Click Me' btnClass='btn btn-info' />
```

This is nice technique to define components and in terms of using that components. It is same. Whether a component is created by functional component or using React.Component(). We can use that component by same technique by:

`<ComponentName propName='Prop value, you can also pass function within props.' />`

Composing Components Multiple Times:

In react, a button, a form, a screen, an image or anything is a component, we can render a component multiples times:

```
import React from 'react';
import ReactDOM from 'react-dom';

function Message(props) {
  return (
    <div>
      {props.text}
    </div>
  );
}

ReactDOM.render(
  <div>
    <Message text='You got a message from John' />
```

```
    <Message text='You got a message from Ali' />
    <Message text='You got a message from Sarah' />
    <Message text='You got a message from Janie' />
  </div>
)
```

This will print Message component multiple times with different text. Even components can be split into very smaller components, we can take this comment example;

```
import React from 'react';
import ReactDOM from 'react-dom';

function Author(props) {
  return (
    <div>
      <strong>{props.name}</strong>
    </div>
  );
}

function CommentText(props) {
  return (
    <div>
      <p>
        {props.comment}
      </p>
```

```jsx
      </div>
    );
  }

  function CommentActions(props) {
    return (
      <div>
        <a>Edit</a>
        <a>Like</a>
        <a>Delete</a>
      </div>
    );
  }

  function Comment(props) {
    return (
      <div>
        <Author name={props.author} />
        <CommentText comment={props.comment} />
        <CommentActions />
      </div>
    );
  }

  ReactDOM.render(
    <div>
```

```
    <Comment author='John' comment='Hello' />
    <Comment author='Sarah' comment='How are you' />
  </div>,
  document.getElementById('root')
)
```

So, we have learned how to use components in our app, Again Components are building blocks of our applications, Components can be split into very smaller components. As we have done this task above. The component allows us to split react app into small pieces, like **Navbar, Footer, Main Content, Cards, Images** and etc. Component is building part of application.

Here is the exercise file for printing navbar and hello world

```
<!DOCTYPE html>
<html>
<head>
    <title>React Hello World</title>
</head>
<body>
    <div id="root" ></div>

        <script type="text/javascript" src="react.min.js" ></script>
        <script type="text/javascript" src="react-dom.min.js" ></script>
        <script type="text/javascript" src="browser.min.js" ></script>
            <script type="text/babel">
```

```
var Navbar = React.createClass({
    render: function () {
        return (
            <div className='navbar navbar-default' >
                <div className="navbar-header" >
                    <a className="navbar-brand" >{this.props.brandName}</a>
                </div>
                <div className="collapse navbar-collapse" >
                    <ul className="navbar-nav nav navbar-right" >
                        <li>
                            <a>Home Page</a>
                        </li>
                    </ul>
                </div>
            </div>
        );
    }
});
```

```
var HellWorld = React.createClass({
    render: function() {
        return (
            <div>
                <h1>{this.props.children}</h1>
            </div>
        );
    }
});

var destination = document.querySelector("#root");

ReactDOM.render(
    <div>
        <Navbar brandName="ReactJs" />
        <HellWorld>Hello World</HellWorld>
    </div>,
    destination
);

</script>
</body>
</html>
```

Now we have completed Components chapter and here are some questions that you have to answer.

- What are components?
- What is different between a Component and Functional Component?
- Why component is required in our ReactJS applications?

What are components?

Did you ever hear about Component? Component means a part or element of a larger thing, component is a small part of a big thing. Now apply this to React JS. Components are heart of ReactJS. Components are building part of your application. Let's suppose you have a navigation bar. We can call that navigation bar a component. Everything in our ReactJS component.

What is different between a Component and Functional Component?

I hope you know about functional component. Actually both are same things. There is only one difference. Deceleration is different, but working and using is same.

Why is component required in our ReactJS applications?

As I've told you earlier, the component is the heart of ReactJS. The component is the main feature in ReactJS. ReactJS apps are based on component and ReactJS is based on only components.

Chapter 5
Styling in React

Take out last exercise file from chapter 3 navigation bar. This is what ReactJS is looking right now:

React

- Home Page

HelloWorld

This is not looking good without design. I've added bootstrap classes to navbar. So we will add bootstrap to our project:

\<link rel="stylesheet" type="text/css" href="https://maxcdn.bootstrapcdn.com/bootstrap/3.3.7/css/bootstrap.min.css"\>

This will install bootstrap in ReactJS Now go and create a file with following content and include bootstrap:

\<!DOCTYPE html\>

```html
<html>
<head>
    <title>React Hello World</title>
    <link rel="stylesheet" type="text/css" href="https://maxcdn.bootstrapcdn.com/bootstrap/3.3.7/css/bootstrap.min.css">
</head>
<body>
    <div id="root" ></div>


    <script type="text/javascript" src="react.min.js" ></script>
    <script type="text/javascript" src="react-dom.min.js" ></script>
    <script type="text/javascript" src="browser.min.js" ></script>
        <script type="text/babel">
            var Navbar = React.createClass({
                render: function () {
                    return (
                        <div className='navbar navbar-default' >
                            <div className="navbar-header" >
                                <a className="navbar-brand" >{this.props.brandName}</a>
                            </div>
                            <div className="collapse navbar-collapse" >
```

```
                    <ul className="navbar-nav nav navbar-right" >
                        <li>
                            <a>Home Page</a>
                        </li>
                    </ul>
                </div>
            </div>
        );
    }
});
var HellWorld = React.createClass({
    render: function() {
        return (
            <div>
                <h1>{this.props.children}</h1>
            </div>
        );
    }
});
```

```
            var destination =
document.querySelector("#root");

            ReactDOM.render(
                <div>
                    <Navbar brandName="ReactJs" />
                    <HellWorld>Hello World</HellWorld>
                </div>,
                destination
            );

        </script>
    </body>
</html>
```

Now we have added bootstrap and as we have added bootstrap classes our React will convert into bootstrap theme:

React

HelloWorld

Now we have added bootstrap, and it is working without any problems. Now let's go ahead and write some CSS, create a new style tag in your same HTML file and write down below CSS file:

```
<style type="text/css">
        .navbar {
                background: green;
        }
</style>
```

The navbar will change into green:

HelloWorld

Do you have ever think how to style in React classes or you can how to style in React component. Now let's ahead and create a component called letter that prints letters:

```
var Letter = React.createClass({
    render: function() {
        return (
            <div>
                {this.props.children}
            </div>
        );
    }
});

var destination = document.querySelector("#root");

ReactDOM.render(
    <div>
        <Letter>R</Letter>
        <Letter>e</Letter>
        <Letter>a</Letter>
        <Letter>c</Letter>
        <Letter>t</Letter>
    </div>,
    destination
);
```

This will print letters of React, now go ahead and put each letter to styling, for this we will use object styling in React. Creating an object that defines styling for a letter.

```
var letterStyle = {
        height: 50,
        width: 50,
        background: this.props.bgColor,
        display: 'inline-block',
        fontSize: '25px',
        textAlign: 'center'
};
```

Now use that object in each letter to style it!

```
<span style={letterStyle} >{this.props.children}</span>
```

Now we have provided style to letter and we let's have final style:

```
<!DOCTYPE html>
<html>
<head>
        <title>React Hello World</title>
        <link rel="stylesheet" type="text/css" href="https://maxcdn.bootstrapcdn.com/bootstrap/3.3.7/css/bootstrap.min.css">
        <style type="text/css">
            .navbar {
                background: green;
            }
        </style>
```

```html
</head>
<body>
    <br />
    <div class="container" >
        <div id="root" ></div>
    </div>
    <script type="text/javascript" src="react.min.js" ></script>
    <script type="text/javascript" src="react-dom.min.js" ></script>
    <script type="text/javascript" src="browser.min.js" ></script>
    <script type="text/babel">
        var Letter = React.createClass({
            render: function() {
                var letterStyle = {
                    height: 50,
                    width: 50,
                    background: this.props.bgColor,
                    display: 'inline-block',
                    fontSize: '25px',
                    textAlign: 'center'
                };
                return (
                    <span style={letterStyle}>{this.props.children}</span>
                );
            }
        });
```

```
            var destination =
document.querySelector("#root");

            ReactDOM.render(
                <div>
                    <Letter bgColor="red"
>R</Letter>
                    <Letter bgColor="green"
>e</Letter>
                    <Letter bgColor="blue"
>a</Letter>
                    <Letter bgColor="pink"
>c</Letter>
                    <Letter
bgColor="purple">t</Letter>
                </div>,
                destination
            );

        </script>
</body>
</html>
```

Now copy this whole content and this will greet your app with:

We have successfully styled our letter.

Following things to remember in React component level style;

- Every property is written in camel case if in CSS it has dash (-).
    - "text-overflow" can be written as textOverflow.
    - "table-layout" can be written as tableLayout.
    - "font-variant" can be written as fontVariant.
    - "font-style" can be written as fontStyle.
    - "font-size" can be written as fontSize.
    - "z-index" can be written as zIndex.
    - "background-color" can be written as backgroundColor.
- We can also use components props to make style automatic, as we did in this example:
    - background: this.props.bgColor,

As we have completed this chapter, here are some questions that I wanted to ask from you:

- Why Object based styling is required in React?

- Is there any npm package for ReactJS Styling?

Why Object based styling is required in React?

This is comes to rescue when we need to update CSS when view changes. For example, we need to set background blue on hover on circle. We can update our CSS to blue when visitor hovers on a circle using events.

Is there any npm package for ReactJS Styling?

Yes there is a NPM package for ReactJS styling to increase ReactJS styling that makes it easier to style on ReactJS. The name of package is react-styling. We can install this package by:

Chapter conclusion

As we plunge further and take in more about React, you'll see a few more situations where React does things very any other way than what we've been told is the right method for getting things done on the web. In this instructional exercise, we saw React advancing inline styles in JavaScript as an approach to style content rather than utilizing CSS style rules. Prior, we took a gander at JSX and how the total of your UI can be pronounced in JavaScript utilizing a XML-like linguistic structure that looks like HTML.

In these cases, in the event that you look further underneath the surface, the explanations behind why React veers from customary way of thinking bodes well. Building applications with their exceptionally complex UI necessities requires another method for comprehending them. HTML, CSS, and JavaScript procedures that most likely appeared well and good when managing website pages and records may not be pertinent in the web application world.

So, you should pick and pick the strategies that bode well for your circumstance. While I am one-sided towards ReactJS method for taking care of our UI improvement issues, I'll do my best to highlight substitute or traditional techniques also. Binds that back to what we saw here, utilizing CSS style rules with your React content is absolutely OK as long as you settled on the choice knowing the things you pick up and additionally lose thusly.

Chapter 6
Building Complex Components

We have created very tiny application so far, in this chapter we will take a free design from online and implement it in our react app. Again, let me explain again what components are:

- Components are building parts of your application.
- Every part of application is a component. Navigation bar, footer, chat box, messages in chat box, card and every small item is a component.
- Components helps also to split applications into very small parts.`
- In this chapter, we take a free landing page from online and we will convert it into react app.

NOTE: "In this chapter we have used, NODE JS based react app to create a example. You will need to go to installation part again understand again how to install react using Node JS". You can get Node JS here according to your system architecture.

You can download this template here or you can use content from here because every image, CSS file and JS file is free on this theme, so you download this theme and use that content for free as I've did. from start bootstrap. On completion of this chapter you will finally learn how to build complex components. Once you extract the downloaded file, you will have following folder structure.

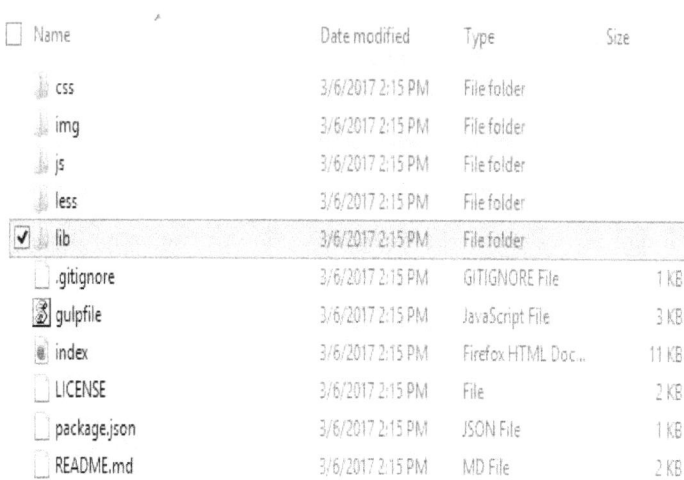

Following folder are not required, you can delete them.

- /less
- package.json
- Readme.md
- gulpfile.js
- license
- .gitignore

Now copy **img/**, **js/** and **lib/** folder to src folder, **img/** folder should be on both src **folder/** and **public/** folder, We will split html into components. Awesome right!

Now delete all old components and styles CSS files from src folder, now go and review the theme we downloaded, you will following section, we can call them components.

1. Navbar
2. Welcome Section
3. Download
4. Features
5. Call out
6. Social
7. Footer

So far, we have 7 components, we will create 7 folders for different components instead of putting them in single folder and create following files:

- navbar/navbar.js
- welcome/welcome.js
- download/download.js
- features/features.js
- callout/callout.js
- social/social.js
- footer/footer.js

navbar/navbar.js

import React from 'react';

```
export default class Navbar extends React.Component{
    render() {
        return (
            <nav id="mainNav" class="navbar navbar-default navbar-fixed-top">
                // src/navbar/navbar.js
            </nav>
        )
    }
}
```

welcome/welcome.js

```
import React from 'react';

export default class Welcome extends React.Component{
    render() {
        return (
            <header>
                // src/welcome/welcome.js
            </header>
        );
    }
}
```

download/download.js

```jsx
import React from 'react';

export default class Downlaod extends React.Component{
    render() {
        return (
            <section id="download" class="download bg-primary text-center">
                // src/download/download.js
            </section>
        );
    }
}
```

features/features.js

```jsx
import React from 'react';

export default class Features extends React.Component{
    render() {
        return (
            <section id="features" class="features">
                // src/features/features.js
            </section>
```

```
        );
    }
}
```

callout/callout.js

```
import React from 'react';

export default class Callout extends React.Component{
    render() {
        return (
            <section class="cta">

            </section>
        );
    }
}
```

social/social.js

```
import React from 'react';

export default class Social extends React.Component{
    render() {
        return (
```

```
                <section id="contact" class="contact bg-primary">
                    // src/social/social.js
        </section>
            );
        }
}
```

footer/footer.js

```
import React from 'react';

export default class Footer extends React.Component{
    render() {
        return (
            <footer>
                // src/footer/footer.js
            </footer>
        );
    }
}
```

I've attached file destination for every component so you can find rest of the content at given path.

Now import and use these component into index.js to build the theme.

src/index.js

import React from 'react';
import ReactDOM from 'react-dom';
import Callout from './callout/callout.js';
import Download from './download/download.js';
import Features from './features/features.js';
import Footer from './footer/footer.js';
import Navbar from './navbar/navbar.js';
import Social from './social/social.js';
import Welcome from './welcome/welcome.js';
import 'bootstrap/dist/css/bootstrap.css';

var Content = function () {
  return (

      <Nabvar />
      <Welcome />
      <Download />
      <Features />
      <Callout />
      <Social />
      <Footer />

  );

}

ReactDOM.render(<Content />,document.getElementById('root'))

This should compile successfully and our app should look like this:

This is without CSS, as we have placed our CSS folder in src folder. Now import following necessary files:

- Bootstrap Framework
- Font Awesome
- Theme CSS File

Now go ahead and create a CSS file called custom.css in src folder with following content:

```
.navbar .navbar-brand {
        color: #000 !important;
}
.navbar li a {
        color: #000 !important;
}
.navbar {
        background: white;
}
```

After importing all necessary files **index.js** file should look like this:

src/index.js

```
import React from 'react';
import ReactDOM from 'react-dom';
import Callout from './callout/callout.js';
import Download from './download/download.js';
import Features from './features/features.js';
import Footer from './footer/footer.js';
import Navbar from './navbar/navbar.js';
import Social from './social/social.js';
import Welcome from './welcome/welcome.js';
import 'jquery/dist/jquery.min.js';
```

```
import 'bootstrap/dist/css/bootstrap.css';
import "./css/new-age.css";
import './custom.css';
import './lib/font-awesome/css/font-awesome.css';

var Content = function () {
  return (
    <div>
      <Navbar />
      <Welcome />
      <Download />
      <Features />
      <Callout />
      <Social />
      <Footer />

    </div>
  );
}

ReactDOM.render(<Content />,document.getElementById('root'))
```

So, we have built many components and successfully converted a theme into react, following things we have learned in this chapter:

- Splitting our application into components, so we can easily navigate to your code and understand and change them.
- How to convert a Theme into ReactJS.
- Installing and Importing Bootstrap and other libraries.
- React allows us to split our application into very small pieces using component.
- As you can in /src/navbar/navbar.js, There is Bootstrap Navbar header, we can create a small component for header:

src/navbar/navbar.js

```
import React from 'react';

class NavbarHeader extends React.Component{
    render() {
        return (
            <div className="navbar-header">
                <button type="button" className="navbar-toggle collapsed" data-toggle="collapse" data-target="#bs-example-navbar-collapse-1">
                    <span className="sr-only">Toggle navigation</span> Menu <i className="fa fa-bars"></i>
                </button>
                <a className="navbar-brand page-scroll" href="#page-top">Start Bootstrap</a>
            </div>
        );
```

```jsx
        }
}

export default class Navbar extends React.Component{
    render() {
        return (
            <nav id="mainNav" className="navbar navbar-default navbar-fixed-top">
                <div className="container">
                    <NavbarHeader />
                    <div className="collapse navbar-collapse" id="bs-example-navbar-collapse-1">
                        <ul className="nav navbar-nav navbar-right">
                            <li>
                                <a className="page-scroll" href="#download">Download</a>
                            </li>
                            <li>
                                <a className="page-scroll" href="#features">Features</a>
                            </li>
                            <li>
                                <a className="page-scroll" href="#contact">Contact</a>
                            </li>
                        </ul>
```

```
              </div>
            </div>
          </nav>
        )
      }
}
```

We have used component NavbarHeader as <NavbarHeader />. Go ahead and see how application looks like.

As we have completed here are some questions:

- How to make components interact each other?
- How to make focus an input in component after render?

How to make components interact each other?

Communication between different parts of an application is important. In react this can be done by props. We can pass functions or values from one component to another by using props.

How to make focus an input text in component after render?

We can make an input focus in component after render by two ways:

First Way:

Simply we can use

<input autoFocus name=...

On input to make it focus after render.

Second Way:

We can make an input focus after by React Using:

<input ref={input => input && input.focus()} />

Chapter conclusion:

As we have completed our chapter Components and we have learned how to create ReactJS components. As told I earlier, components are building parts of our application and they are heart of application. In next chapter we will learn how to install jQuery plugins in our ReactJS applications.

Chapter 7
Installing and using jQuery Plugins in React

So, we have learned how to create components, how to create an app, styling in ReactJS, in this chapter we will learn how to install jQuery plugins and using them. So, let me tell you what is JQuery? JQuery is a JavaScript library, JQuery has dozens of functions to deal with DOM, hiding them, removing them, and there are thousands of plugins out there for JQuery. JQuery makes easier to make changes to DOM.

95% percent of plugins are free to install and using them on our website. JQuery plugins can be easily embed to any web app.

In this chapter, we will learn how to install and use JQuery plugins in React app. To run a JQuery plugin in react app, we will need jQuery in our application.

Go ahead and create a new fresh application. Remove all files from src folder keep index.js and App.js with following content:

src/index.js

```
import React from 'react';
import ReactDOM from 'react-dom';
import App from './App';

ReactDOM.render(<App />, document.getElementById('root'));
```

src/App.js

```
import React from 'react';

export default class App extends React.Component {
    render() {
        return (
            <h1>Welcome to my App</h1>
        );
    }
}
```

This will print Welcome to my App on the screen. Now let's go ahead and download JQuery:

```
-> npm i jquery --save
```

We will use JQuery SlimScroll by Rochal. Now create a file called **slimscroll.js** that will convert body scrollbar into SlimScroll bar. As we have installed JQuery we can import it and using jquery.getScript() function we can import a SlimScroll from a CDN and run function after script.

src/slimscroll.js

```javascript
import React from 'react';
import $ from 'jquery';
window.jQuery = $;

export default class Slimscroll extends React.Component{
    render() {
        this.h();
        return (
            <div>

            </div>
        );
    }
    h() {

        $.getScript('https://cdnjs.cloudflare.com/ajax/libs/jQuery-slimScroll/1.3.8/jquery.slimscroll.min.js', function(data, textStatus) {
            $("body").slimScroll({
                size: '8px',
                width: '100%',
                height: '100%',
                color: '#ff4800',
                allowPageScroll: true,
                alwaysVisible: true
            });
```

            });
        }
    }

This will change browser scrollbar into something like this:

Now we have learned how to use jQuery plugins in React Apps. Go ahead and try another plugin. If you wondering how to add other plugins. The way is same as we did in this demo. First you have to install jQuery and then use $.getScript() to require script from a location. On $.getScript() callback, initialize your plugin as we did in example.

Now we have completed our chapter and here some questions:

- What is jQuery and why it is used?
- What is $.ajax() and how to use it with ReactJS?

What is jQuery and why it is used?

JQuery is a JavaScript library. It is very fast, very small and feature rich. It makes easy to play with DOM and its manipulation. Event handling, animation and Ajax becomes easier with jQuery. JQuery is used to make web applications very fast and that are easy to change.

What is $.ajax() and how to use it with ReactJS?

$.ajax() is a Jquery function that allows us to create make Ajax calls. It is very easy to use it with a Ajax. If you want to have Ajax feature in our ReactJS application. Then I recommend to use $.ajax() with your ReactJS application. As we bind component functions to component elements like button, input or form like click, hover or submit. We can send ajax request on that function.

Chapter Conclusion:

Now we have completed this chapter and we have learned how to install jQuery plugins. This chapter covers how to install jQuery plugins in our ReactJS App. Now let's move to chapter 8 and we will learn how to transfer data and functions between components.

Chapter 8

Transferring data and functions through Components

We have learned how to create components and using them in our ReactJS application. Did you've ever think how to pass parameters to components in React, as you know we can data through functions like this;

functionName(value1,value2);

As you know we can call components by **<MyComponent />**, But how to pass data to a component? We can pass data through functions as defined above. We can call components in React like html tag, simply we can pass data through it by attributes:

<MyComponent name='John Doe' />

In this chapter, we will learn again how to create components and pass values and functions to it. In this chapter, let's create a Button Component to show how to pass data and functions to components in React, First install a fresh React plain application.

index.html

```
var Button = React.createClass({
    render: function() {
    return (
        <button>{this.props.children}</button>
        );
    }
});

var destination = document.querySelector("#root");

ReactDOM.render(
    <div>
        <Button>Click me</Button>
    </div>,
    destination
);
```

This will print a button:

[Click me]

This will print a button, this is a static button that will do nothing. As we have passed child as button text, this is also type of props. Now go ahead add on click attribute to button:

`<button onClick={this.props.onClick} >{this.props.children}</button>`

Now create a function and while calling button component. Pass that function to button component

```html
<!DOCTYPE html>
<html>
<head>
    <title>React Hello World</title>
    <link rel="stylesheet" type="text/css" href="https://maxcdn.bootstrapcdn.com/bootstrap/3.3.7/css/bootstrap.min.css">
</head>
<body>
    <br />
    <div class="container" >
        <div id="root" ></div>
    </div>
    <script type="text/javascript" src="react.min.js" ></script>
    <script type="text/javascript" src="react-dom.min.js" ></script>
    <script type="text/javascript" src="browser.min.js" ></script>
    <script type="text/babel">
        var Button = React.createClass({
            render: function() {
                return (
                    <button onClick={this.props.onClick} >{this.props.children}</button>
                );
            }
```

```
        });

            var destination =
document.querySelector("#root");

            var buttonClick = function () {
                alert(1);
            }

            ReactDOM.render(
                <div>
                    <Button onClick={buttonClick}>Click me</Button>
                </div>,
                destination
            );

        </script>
    </body>
</html>
```

While calling component I have passed a function to that component. If everything works fine, we will be greeted with a button, after clicking on that button, JavaScript will make an alert.

Let's make something. Now we have learned how to pass functions and values to components in React.

Quiz:

Go ahead and create to do app using React features learned so far. This can be achieved by doing following things:

- Creating a component that holds form and functions to store todo items.
    - A function that returns states.
        - All states
            - todoInput - contains input
            - todoLists - contains all todo lists.
        - Functions
            - updateInput - updates value to states right after a change is made on input
            - save – this function stores new todo list, alerts a message called "Please write something" if visito
- Creating a component that lists all todo items.

Here is the app:

<!DOCTYPE html>

```html
<html>
<head>
    <title>React Hello World</title>
    <link rel="stylesheet" type="text/css" href="https://maxcdn.bootstrapcdn.com/bootstrap/3.3.7/css/bootstrap.min.css">
</head>
<body>
    <br />
    <div class="container" >
        <div id="root" ></div>
    </div>
    <script type="text/javascript" src="react.min.js" ></script>
    <script type="text/javascript" src="react-dom.min.js" ></script>
    <script type="text/javascript" src="browser.min.js" ></script>
    <script type="text/babel">
        var Todo = React.createClass({
            getInitialState: function () {
                return {
                    todoInput: "",
                    todoList: [],
                }
            },
            updateInput: function (e) {
                this.setState({todoInput: e.target.value});
            },
            : function (e) {
```

```jsx
        e.preventDefault();
        if (this.state.todoInput) {
            var oldTodos = this.state.todoList;
            oldTodos.push([this.state.todoInput]);
            this.setState({todoInput: ""});
        } else {
            alert("Please type something");
        }
    },
    render: function() {
        return (
            <div>
                <form onSubmit={this.save} >
                    <h3>Add a todo</h3>
                    <input className="form-control" value={this.state.todoInput} onChange={this.updateInput} type="text" />
                    <br />
                    <button className="btn btn-info" >Save</button>
                    <hr />
                    <NumberList list={this.state.todoList} ></NumberList>
                </form>
            </div>
        );
    }
});
```

```jsx
function NumberList(props) {
    const list = props.list;
    if (list.length == 0) {
        var listItems = "No Items Right Now ";
    } else {
        var listItems = list.map((todoItem) =>
            <li key={todoItem.toString()}>
                <a>{todoItem}</a>
            </li>
        );
    }
    return (
        <ul className="nav " >{listItems}</ul>
    );
}


var destination = document.querySelector("#root");

ReactDOM.render(
    <div>
        <Todo></Todo>
    </div>,
    destination
);
</script>
```

</body>
</html>

This will print todo app with bootstrap included. Let's suppose a moment in which we may have no todo lists and our app will render a message with no todo list:

After adding some items, ReactJS will render our items in following way:

Now we have working example of Todo List, Now take out the code from the example and paste in a html file and open in your browser while including react, react-dom and browser min js.

If you successfully paste this code, this file will greet you with a working example of todo list.

We have learned following things in this chapter

- Components.
- Functional Components.
- Intro to states (You will learn more about states in near chapter).
- Creating a todo lists.
- Saving our data in Arrays.
- Retrieving data from Arrays and listing it in views.

Here are some questions:

- **How to pass a function to a component?**
- **How to pass a value to a component?**

How to pass a function to a component?

We can pass a function to a component by props. React allows us to pass a function to a component, we can pass a function to a component by:

`<BlueButton onclick={this.blueButtonClick} ></BlueButton>`

How to pass a value to a component?

This is same as passing a function to a component as above did. We can pass a value by:

`<Alert message={this.state.alertMessage} ></Alert>`

Chapter conclusion:

Now we have successfully completed this chapter and we learned how to transfer values and function using components props. Now let's move to chapter Dealing with states.

Chapter 9
Dealing with States

If you know working of properties, you will probably know how to work with states. What is different between States and Properties?

Properties are passed from outside of component. Properties are considered immutable once they set in many application we want our application to update as visitor makes changes to our site.

States: We can store data in components by something well know **states**. We can remove and update value of states, according to view changes.

It means we can change views of a component according to some state. As defined above clearly. States make our application dynamic as visitor tries to make changes in our app. Using states, we can store our data in components and using API we can store them on database. Like Vue js React does not update value of states, we have to write functions that update value of state.

```
onChange(e) {
  this.setState({
    todoInput: e.target.value
  });
```

}

When a state is changed in component, the component renders itself again. Everything is done by react itself at back.

Let's go ahead and create a fresh application, now go to src/**app.js,** To create new state in constructor function:

```
constructor(props) {
   super(props);
   this.state = {
      message: "Hello World"
   };
}
```

For React.createClass()

```
getInitialState: function () {
   return {
      todoInput: "",
      todoList: [],
   }
},
```

I have assigned a state called message, All states comes in an object with values, throughout component, all will be available on this.state, If we console.log state we will have following result in console:

Object {message: "Hello World"}

I have explained it already told you that states is an object that contains values. To print this message, we can:

```html
<!DOCTYPE html>
<html>
<head>
   <title>React Hello World</title>
</head>
<body>
   <br />
   <div class="container" >
      <div id="root" ></div>
   </div>
   <script type="text/javascript" src="react.min.js" ></script>
   <script type="text/javascript" src="react-dom.min.js" ></script>
   <script type="text/javascript" src="browser.min.js" ></script>
   <script type="text/babel">

      var App = React.createClass({
         getInitialState: function () {
```

```
        return {
            message: "Hello World"
        }
      },
      render: function () {
        return (
          <div>
              Welcome to Todo App | {this.state.message}
          </div>
        );
      }
    });



    var destination = document.querySelector("#root");

    ReactDOM.render(
      <div>
         <App></App>
      </div>,
      destination
    );
  </script>
</body>
</html>
```

If this code compiles successfully we will be greeted with:

Welcome to Todo App | Hello World

Let's create a button that will update the value of message and also create a that will change value of message state.

```html
<!DOCTYPE html>
<html>
<head>
    <title>React Hello World</title>
</head>
<body>
    <br />
    <div class="container" >
        <div id="root" ></div>
    </div>
    <script type="text/javascript" src="react.min.js" ></script>
    <script type="text/javascript" src="react-dom.min.js" ></script>
    <script type="text/javascript" src="browser.min.js" ></script>
    <script type="text/babel">

        var App = React.createClass({
```

```
getInitialState: function () {
  return {
    message: "Hello World"
  }
},
changeValue: function () {
  this.setState({
    message: "Value Changed!"
  });
},

render: function () {
  return (
    <div>
        Welcome to Todo App | {this.state.message}
        <br />
        <button onClick={this.changeValue} >Click Me</button> to change value
    </div>
  );
}
});


var destination = document.querySelector("#root");
```

```
    ReactDOM.render(
        <div>
            <App></App>
        </div>,
        destination
    );
    </script>
</body>
</html>
```

After click on button the value will be change to **'Value Changed!'**

Welcome to Todo App | Value Changed!
Click Me to change value

As you can that image, the value of state is changed!

States comes with components, We can make our components dynamic using states in ReactJS, in JavaScript,, state management is very big topic. We can change our view using states. According to Wikipedia about state management it says:

Management of state of many interfaces that controls text fields, buttons, radio inputs etc. In this user interface State Management is used to control other user interfaces.

This explains very briefly about state management, changing view according to state is called state management.

Another popular state management library, Redux is clearly the most popular of the Flux implementations, an architecture championed by Facebook as a system for managing state globally in React or other frontend libraries. 87% of users had heard of Redux, which is pretty incredible given it is barely a year old and competing for mindshare with a host of other Flux implementations (as we'll see below).

Redux is very popular state management software. For Vue js it Vuex. Redux is created by software engineer at Facebook to control state management in ReactJS,, later this tool become more popular to control state management in ReactJS, We will learn Redux in future chapter. Specially served for Vue JS.

Here are some questions:

- How to store components states?
- How to dynamically create components?

For both questions we have same answer that shows how to store components in components and how to dynamically create components. It is a tricky to store components and create components dynamically. This is how we can store components in states and create components dynamically:

```html
<!DOCTYPE html>
<html>
<head>
  <title>React Hello World</title>
</head>
<body>
  <br />
  <div class="container" >
    <div id="root" ></div>
  </div>
  <script type="text/javascript" src="react.min.js" ></script>
  <script type="text/javascript" src="react-dom.min.js" ></script>
  <script type="text/javascript" src="browser.min.js" ></script>
  <script type="text/babel">

    class App extends React.Component{
      render() {
        var colors = ['red','blue','yellow','pink','lightgreen',"lightblue","#eee","#42a"];
        var circles = [];
        for (var i = 0; i < colors.length; i++) {
          var color = colors[i];
          var c = <Circle key={i} bgColor={colors[i]} />;
          circles.push(c);
```

```
      }
    return (
      <div>
        <h3>Hello World</h3>
        {circles}
      </div>
    );
  }
}
class Circle extends React.Component{
  render() {
    var circleStyles= {
      display: 'inline-block',
      background: this.props.bgColor,
      height: 20,
      width: 20,
      borderRadius: "50%",
      textAlign: "center",
      marginRight: '5'
    }
    return (
    <div style={circleStyles} ></div>
    );
  }
}
```

```
        var destination = document.querySelector("#root");

        ReactDOM.render(
            <div>
                <App></App>
            </div>,
            destination
        );
    </script>
</body>
</html>
```

This will help us to store components in store and create components dynamically.

Chapter 10
Integrating React With Yii 2

Let me tell you what Yii is, Yii is a superior PHP structure best to develop Web 2.0 applications. Yii accompanies rich elements: MVC, DAO/ActiveRecord, I18N/L10N, reserving, verification and part based get to control, platform, testing, and so forth. It can diminish your improvement time fundamentally. For this tutorial we will need a web server to run PHP as well as Yii2, Current version of Yii is 2.00 version. Go ahead and download Yii2 from here. After downloading Yii2 project. Extract the zip to a folder into www folder under Wamp or Xampp folder. Open the extracted folder in and run **init** in cmd.

```
C:\wamp\www\react\Yii>init
Yii Application Initialization Tool v1.0

Which environment do you want the application to be initialized in?

  [0] Development
  [1] Production

  Your choice [0-1, or "q" to quit]
```

Write 1 and write y then hit enter. This will initialize Yii project for you. Now go to http://localhost/path/to/yii2/frontend/web// to see if it works. If it works, Your screen will be greeted with:

Now go to **frontend/assets/AppAssets.php** and add ReactJS:

```
<?php

namespace frontend\assets;

use yii\web\AssetBundle;

/**
```

* Main frontend application asset bundle.
 */
class AppAsset extends AssetBundle
{
    public $basePath = '@webroot';
    public $baseUrl = '@web';
    public $css = [
        'css/site.css',
    ];
    public $js = [
        "https://fb.me/react-15.1.0.min.js",
        "https://fb.me/react-dom-15.1.0.min.js",
        "https://cdnjs.cloudflare.com/ajax/libs/babel-core/5.8.23/browser.min.js",
    ];
    public $depends = [
        'yii\web\YiiAsset',
        'yii\bootstrap\BootstrapAsset',
    ];
}

For JavaScript, we have now added ReactJS into our Yii project, and now go ahead and do some coding. Create a folder in **/frontend/web/js/react-components**, Create a folder in react-components called ReactJS that will import all react components. We have include this file in **frontend/layouts/main.php,** after **<?php $this->endBody() ?>**

```html
<script type="text/jsx" src="js/react-components/reactjsjs"
></script>
```

We have to use JSX platform to run make our Yii project compatible with ReactJS, now go to console and see If there is a error and make sure your JavaScript added files look alike this:

```html
<script src="/react/yii/frontend/web/assets/922d48f2/jquery.js"></script>
<script src="/react/yii/frontend/web/assets/a08992ed/yii.js"></script>
<script src="https://fb.me/react-15.1.0.min.js"></script>
<script src="https://fb.me/react-dom-15.1.0.min.js"></script>
<script src="https://cdnjs.cloudflare.com/ajax/libs/babel-core/5.8.23/browser.min.js"></script>
<script src="/react/yii/frontend/web/assets/1abd151d/js/bootstrap.js"></script>
<script type="text/jsx" src="js/react-components/reactjsjs" ></script>
```

I hope there will be no errors in console. Now go to **frontend/web/js/react-components/**, and write ReactJS with following content:

```
class HelloWorld extends React.Component{
    render() {
        return (
```

```
            <div className='jumbotron text-center' >
                <h1>Welcome</h1>
                <p>
                    Welcome to My Yii project powered by React Js
                </p>
            </div>
        );
    }
}

ReactDOM.render(<HelloWorld />,document.getElementById('helloWorld'));
```

Now go to frontend/views/site/index.php and remove everything from there and put a new content in it:

```
<?php
$this->title = 'My Yii Application';
?>
<div class="site-index">
    <div id="helloWorld"></div>
</div>
```

You will be greeted with:

It means we have successfully integrated react into our Yii project. Now we can use all React resources in our Yii app. Now convert the navbar into React component. Now go to frontend/web/js/reactjs and create a component for Navbar.Js

frontend/web/js/reactjsJs

```
class Navbar extends React.Component{
    render() {
        return (
            <div className='navbar navbar-inverse navbar-fixed-top' >
                <div className='container' >
                    <div className='navbar-header' >
                        <a className='navbar-brand' >ReactYii</a>
```

```
                        </div>
                        <div className='navbar-collapse collapse' >
                            <ul className="nav navbar-right navbar-nav" >
                                <li><a>Home</a></li>
                                <li><a>About</a></li>
                                <li><a>Contact</a></li>
                            </ul>
                        </div>
                    </div>
                </div>
            );
        }
    }

ReactDOM.render(<Navbar />,document.getElementById('navbar'));
```

Now remove old navbar from **frontend/layouts/main.php** and add a div with id navbar

```
<div id="navbar" ></div>
```

This will greet us with something like this:

Welcome

Welcome to My Yii project powered by React Js

Now we have integrated ReactJS into Yii project. Here are some questions:

- What is Yii and why it is used for?
- How to include Yii with Node JS based ReactJS Application?

What is Yii and why it is used for?

Yii is PHP framework and it is a high-performance component-based PHP framework best for Web 2.0 development. Yii has frontend and backend support. I mean Yii gives us frontend website as well as admin panel for our website. Yii was originally launched on 2008. In this chapter we have integrated Yii with React JS in chapter.

Yii is used to develop PHP websites that are fast and scalable. Yii is popular due to easy to learn, easy to understand and well manage framework.

How to include Yii with Node JS based ReactJS Application?

We cannot include Yii into Node JS ReactJS application because Node JS server is completely different from a PHP framework. To achieve this problem. We need two servers. Wampserver and ReactJS (Node JS Based). We will set a path for Yii, such as localhost/yii-project. We can send Ajax requests to this URL to server PHP and MYSQL jobs. You can learn Yii (http://ww.yiiframework.com/)

Chapter Conclusion:

Now we have integrated ReactJS into Yii project. Now go ahead and write some ReactJS code and make your Yii app full of ReactJS. Now go to let's go to chapter Going from data to UI.

Chapter 10
Going from Data to UI

This chapter is about using data to make UI, Making UI interactive by using data in ReactJS Yeah! We can make our UI interactive by using data in ReactJS Let's say we have a circle in plain HTML and CSS,

<div className="circle" ></div>

And css for making it circle

```
.circle {
    display: inline-block;
        background: red;
        height: 20px;
        width: 20px;
        border-radius: 50%;
        text-align: center;
}
.circle.green {
        background: green;
}
.circle.blue {
        background: blue;
```

}

We will need different stylesheet to make circle background different. Like blue, green etc. We will three div tags to make them different in color.

<div className="circle " ></div>
<div className="circle blue" ></div>
<div className="circle green" ></div>

OK, This will print:

Ok It worked! What if you will need 20 circle with different colors or 30 circles with different circles. Are you going to write so much CSS? Ok, let's get rid of this problem by components.

Go ahead and create a fresh react application, and create a component for circle, create a file called circle.js

<!DOCTYPE html>
<html>
<head>
    <title>React Hello World</title>
</head>

```html
<body>
  <br />
  <div class="container" >
    <div id="root" ></div>
  </div>
  <script type="text/javascript" src="react.min.js" ></script>
  <script type="text/javascript" src="react-dom.min.js" ></script>
  <script type="text/javascript" src="browser.min.js" ></script>
  <script type="text/babel">

    class App extends React.Component{
      render() {
        return (
          <div>
            <h3>Hello World</h3>
            <Circle />
            <Circle />
          </div>
        );
      }
    }
    class Circle extends React.Component{
      render() {
        var circleStyles= {
        display: 'inline-block',
        background: 'red',
        height: 20,
```

```
            width: 20,
            borderRadius: "50%",
            textAlign: "center",
            marginRight: '5'
          }
          return (
            <div style={circleStyles} ></div>
          );
        }
      }


      var destination = document.querySelector("#root");

      ReactDOM.render(
        <div>
          <App></App>
        </div>,
        destination
      );
    </script>
  </body>
</html>
```

If this compiles successfully, ReactJS will greet us with two circles:

Hello World

This compiles our circles, as I have said earlier we will need a feature that will compiles our circle in different circles. Props save us from this problem.

Circle Component

```
class Circle extends React.Component{
  render() {
    var circleStyles= {
      display: 'inline-block',
      background: this.props.bgColor,
      height: 20,
      width: 20,
      borderRadius: "50%",
      textAlign: "center",
      marginRight: '5'
    }
    return (
      <div style={circleStyles} ></div>
    );
```

        }
    }

Instead of red I have changed the background red to this.props.bgColor, before rendering component. We have to pass a background color to circle component,

App Component

```
class Circle extends React.Component{
    render() {
        var circleStyles= {
            display: 'inline-block',
            background: this.props.bgColor,
            height: 20,
            width: 20,
            borderRadius: "50%",
            textAlign: "center",
            marginRight: '5'
        }
        return (
            <div style={circleStyles} ></div>
        );
    }
}
```

This will print circles in different colors.

Hello World

This successfully created our circles, Instead of printing components like this:

```
<Circle bgColor='red' />
<Circle bgColor='blue' />
<Circle bgColor='yellow' />
<Circle bgColor='pink' />
<Circle bgColor='lightgreen' />
```

Let's create an object before rendering and run for loop for colors. In every for loop. Create component and assign a background color. Then use that variable in view.

App Component

```
class App extends React.Component{
    render() {
        var colors = ['red','blue','yellow','pink','lightgreen'];
```

```
var circles = [];
for (var i = 0; i < colors.length; i++) {
        var color = colors[i];
        var c = <Circle key={i} bgColor={colors[i]} />;
        circles.push(c);
}
return (
        <div>
                <h3>Hello World</h3>
                {circles}
        </div>
        );
    }
}
```

This will print the same result.

Hello World

Now if we don't need to use component to add another circle to our app. We will to push another color in our array:

App Component

```
class App extends React.Component{
    render() {
        var colors = ['red','blue','yellow','pink','lightgreen',"lightblue","#eee","#42a"];
        var circles = [];
        for (var i = 0; i < colors.length; i++) {
            var color = colors[i];
            var c = <Circle key={i} bgColor={colors[i]} />;
            circles.push(c);
        }
        return (
            <div>
                <h3>Hello World</h3>
                {circles}
            </div>
        );
    }
}
```

A question! How can you add a new circle on button click?

This will print more circles. This explains how to use data to form UI in ReactJS we have successfully created our circles.

This is our final exercise file, Now copy this file and if this works fine, you will be greeted with circles on your screen!

```html
<!DOCTYPE html>
<html>
<head>
   <title>React Hello World</title>
</head>
<body>
   <br />
   <div class="container" >
      <div id="root" ></div>
   </div>
   <script type="text/javascript" src="react.min.js" ></script>
   <script type="text/javascript" src="react-dom.min.js" ></script>
   <script type="text/javascript" src="browser.min.js" ></script>
   <script type="text/babel">

      class App extends React.Component{
         render() {
            var colors = ['red','blue','yellow','pink','lightgreen',"lightblue","#eee","#42a"];
            var circles = [];
            for (var i = 0; i < colors.length; i++) {
               var color = colors[i];
               var c = <Circle key={i} bgColor={colors[i]} />;
               circles.push(c);
            }
            return (
```

```jsx
      <div>
        <h3>Hello World</h3>
        {circles}
      </div>
    );
  }
}
class Circle extends React.Component{
  render() {
    var circleStyles= {
      display: 'inline-block',
      background: this.props.bgColor,
      height: 20,
      width: 20,
      borderRadius: "50%",
      textAlign: "center",
      marginRight: '5'
    }
    return (
      <div style={circleStyles} ></div>
    );
  }
}

var destination = document.querySelector("#root");
```

```
    ReactDOM.render(
        <div>
            <App></App>
        </div>,
        destination
    );
</script>
</body>
</html>
```

Answer to question: I have asked question **"How can you add a new circle on button click?"** You can create a function that adds a new circle, here is how you can do it, create a constructor like this:

```
constructor(props) {
    super(props);
    this.state = {
        myCircles: []
    };

    this.addCircle = this.addCircle.bind(this);
    var colors =
['red','blue','yellow','pink','lightgreen',"lightblue","#eee","#42a"];
    var circles = [];
    for (var i = 0; i < colors.length; i++) {
```

```
        var color = colors[i];
        var c = <Circle key={i} bgColor={colors[i]} />;
        circles.push(c);
    }

    this.state = {
        myCircles: circles
    };
}
```

That automatically adds circles to your web app. This will print same result as it did before. Now add a button and create a function that adds a new circle to circles array found instates

```
<!DOCTYPE html>
<html>
<head>
    <title>React Hello World</title>
</head>
<body>
    <br />
    <div class="container" >
        <div id="root" ></div>
    </div>
    <script type="text/javascript" src="react.min.js" ></script>
    <script type="text/javascript" src="react-dom.min.js" ></script>
```

```
<script type="text/javascript" src="browser.min.js" ></script>
<script type="text/babel">

    class App extends React.Component{
        constructor(props) {
            super(props);
            this.state = {
                myCircles: []
            };

            this.addCircle = this.addCircle.bind(this);
            var colors =
['red','blue','yellow','pink','lightgreen','lightblue',"#eee","#42a"];
            var circles = [];
            for (var i = 0; i < colors.length; i++) {
                var color = colors[i];
                var c = <Circle key={i} bgColor={colors[i]} />;
                circles.push(c);
            }

            this.state = {
                myCircles: circles
            };
        }
        render() {
            return (
                <div>
```

```
          <h3>Hello World</h3>
          {this.state.myCircles}
          <br />
          <br />
          <button onClick={this.addCircle} >Add a circle</button>
        </div>
      );
    }
    addCircle() {
      var circles = this.state.myCircles;
      var newCircle = <Circle bgColor='blue' />;
      circles.push(newCircle);
      this.setState({myCircles: circles});
    }
}
class Circle extends React.Component{
    render() {
      var circleStyles= {
        display: 'inline-block',
        background: this.props.bgColor,
        height: 20,
        width: 20,
        borderRadius: "50%",
        textAlign: "center",
        marginRight: '5'
      }
      return (
```

```
          <div style={circleStyles} ></div>
        );
      }
    }


      var destination = document.querySelector("#root");

      ReactDOM.render(
        <div>
          <App></App>
        </div>,
        destination
      );
  </script>
</body>
</html>
```

Now go ahead and you can see a button that adds a new circle on click

Hello World

Here are some questions/quizzes:

- How to define transition for static and hover state?

How to define transition for static and hover state?

When we apply new styles on hover state on an element. The transition does not works. We will need to set a new transition style in CSS. Now set some transition on class. Now set that transition on hover and focus state. Now write that CSS deceleration on an element you want to apply transition.

Chapter Conclusion:

Now we have learned how to style in React. We have learned how to update our style. We can update CSS when view changes. For example, we need to set background blue on hover on circle. We can update our CSS to blue when visitor hovers on a circle using events.

Chapter 12
The Component Lifecycle

Did you ever hear of events in JS? The component life cycle is based on events. We can also say the component life events, When It will be rendered, After It mounts and After It unmounts. React team created these events into methods. Here are following Component lifecycle methods:

- **componentWillMount**: This method is executed before rendering on server side and client side.
- **componentDidMount**: This method is executed after component first renders on the client side only.
- **componentWillReceiveProps**: This method is executed as soon as a component receives props.
- **shouldComponentUpdate**: This method verifies whether a component should update on data changes.
- **componentWillUpdate**: This method executes when a component before renders.
- **componentDidUpdate**: This method executes when a component after renders.
- **componentWillUnmount**: This method executes as soon as a component unmounts.

Let's go ahead and create a fresh directory and create a component called **ComponentLifeCycle.js**. I will put a on click increment example to it, so conosle.log will show the events that are passing.

src/ComponentLifeCycle.js

```
import React from 'react';

class App extends React.Component{

  constructor(props) {
    super(props);

    this.state = {
      data: 0
    }

    this.setNewNumber = this.setNewNumber.bind(this)
  };

  setNewNumber() {
    this.setState({data: this.state.data + 1})
  }

  render() {
    return (
      <div>
```

```
        <button onClick =
{this.setNewNumber}>INCREMENT</button>
        <Content myNumber = {this.state.data}></Content>
      </div>
    );
  }
}

class Content extends React.Component{

  componentWillMount() {
    console.log('Component WILL MOUNT!')
  }

  componentDidMount() {
    console.log('Component DID MOUNT!')
  }

  componentWillReceiveProps(newProps) {
    console.log('Component WILL RECIEVE PROPS!')
  }

  shouldComponentUpdate(newProps, newState) {
    return true;
  }

  componentWillUpdate(nextProps, nextState) {
```

```
    console.log('Component WILL UPDATE!');
}

componentDidUpdate(prevProps, prevState) {
    console.log('Component DID UPDATE!')
}

componentWillUnmount() {
    console.log('Component WILL UNMOUNT!')
}

render() {
    return (
      <div>
        <h3>{this.props.myNumber}</h3>
      </div>
    );
  }
}

export default App;
```

Now go to browser console and see logs, you will see something like this:

Component WILL MOUNT! ComponentLifeCycle.js:13
Component DID MOUNT!   ComponentLifeCycle.js:17

There are many functions in our component but only two functions execute, this is because of events. Other events didn't pass. You can see a button on your app. Go ahead and click on that button, you will see console full of logs.

Here are some questions about the chapter:
- What is component lifecycle?
- What is componentWillMount?

What is component lifecycle?

Every Component has a few "lifecycle techniques" that you can abrogate to run code at specific circumstances all the while. Strategies prefixed with will are called just before something happens, and techniques prefixed with did are called directly in the wake of something happens.

What is componentWillMount?

This method is executed before rendering on server side and client side. The React expects this value as a function to be executed.

Chapter Conclusion:

So we have ended our chapter and we have learned how component life cycle works now let's turn to React Router

Chapter 13
React Router

In this chapter, we will learn building applications using react router. So first, what is Router? A **router** is hardware device designed to receive, analyze and move incoming packets to another network. In frontend, A router which navigates user to different, every JavaScript framework or library has Router option.

- React Router
- Angular Router
- Vue Js Router
- Etc

Router is very important topic. Router in React is based on components. Initially react router is not provided, we have to install react router by following command in Node JS:

npm install --save react-router-dom

This will install react router in our application and we can import react router by:

// using ES6 modules
import { BrowserRouter, Route, Link } from 'react-router-dom'

```js
// using CommonJS modules
var BrowserRouter = require('react-router-dom').BrowserRouter
var Route = require('react-router-dom').Route
var Link = require('react-router-dom').Link
```

In plain html we can install react router by just linking to react router:

```html
<script type="text/javascript" src="path/to/react_router.js" ></script>
```

In this chapter, we will create a small app using React router. Navigation to different URLs like:

1. /
2. /about
3. /contact
4. /login
5. /signup

The above will be our routers, The First one will be our home page, second page will be about us page, third will be contact us page and Fourth and Fifth page will be authentication pages.

Go ahead and create those components, remember in ReactJS the router is based on components

App Component

```
class App extends React.Component {
  render() {
    return (
      <div>
        <Navbar />
        <ReactRouter.Router history={ReactRouter.hashHistory}>
          <ReactRouter.Route path="/" component={Home}>
          </ReactRouter.Route>

          <ReactRouter.Route path="/login" component={Login}>
          </ReactRouter.Route>

          <ReactRouter.Route path="/signup" component={Signup}>
          </ReactRouter.Route>


          <ReactRouter.Route path="/contact" component={Contact}>
          </ReactRouter.Route>


          <ReactRouter.Route path="/about" component={About}>
          </ReactRouter.Route>
```

```
        </ReactRouter.Router>
      </div>
    );
  }
}


var destination = document.querySelector("#root");

ReactDOM.render(
  <div>
    <App></App>
  </div>,
  destination
);
```

Navbar Component

```
class Navbar extends React.Component{
  render() {
    return (
      <div className='navbar navbar-default' >
        <div className='container' >
          <div className='navbar-header' >
            <a className='navbar-brand' >React</a>
          </div>
          <div className='collapse navbar-collapse' >
```

```
                <ul className='navbar-nav nav navbar-right' >
                  <li>
                    <a href="/home" >Home</a>
                  </li>
                  <li>
                    <a href="/about" >About</a>
                  </li>
                  <li>
                    <a href="/contact" >Contact</a>
                  </li>
                  <li>
                    <a href="/login" >Login</a>
                  </li>
                  <li>
                    <a href="/signup" >Signup</a>
                  </li>
                </ul>
              </div>
            </div>
          </div>
      );
    }
  }
```

Home Component

```
class Home extends React.Component{
   render() {
      return (
        <div>
           <div className="container" >
              <div className="col-sm-6 col-sm-offset-3" >
                 <h1>Welcome to our React App</h1>
                 <p>
                    tempor incididunt ut labore et dolore magna aliqua. Ut enim ad minim veniam,
                 </p>
              </div>
           </div>
        </div>
      );
   }
}
```

About Component

```
class About extends React.Component{
   render() {
      return (
```

```jsx
      <div>
        <div className="container" >
          <div className="row" >
            <div className="col-sm-6 col-sm-offset-3" >
              <h1>Welcome to about us page</h1>
              <p>
                Lorem ipsum dolor sit amet, consectetur adipisicing elit, sed do eiusmod
              </p>
            </div>
          </div>
        </div>
      </div>
    );
  }
}
```

Contact Component

```jsx
class Contact extends React.Component{
   render() {
     return (
       <div>
         <div className="container" >
           <div className="row" >
```

```jsx
            <div className="col-sm-6 col-sm-offset-3" >
                <form>
                    <div className="form-group" >
                        <label>Name</label>
                        <input className="form-control" placeholder="name" type="text" ></input>
                    </div>
                    <div className="form-group" >
                        <label>Email</label>
                        <input className="form-control" placeholder="name" type="text" ></input>
                    </div>
                    <div className="form-group" >
                        <label>Message</label>
                        <textarea className="form-control" placeholder="name" type="text" ></textarea>
                    </div>
                    <div className="form-group" >
                        <button className="btn btn-info" >Contact</button>
                    </div>
                </form>
            </div>
        </div>
    </div>
</div>
);
```

        }
}

Signup Component

```
class Signup extends React.Component{
    render() {
        return (
            <div>
                <div className="container" >
                    <div className="row" >
                        <div className="col-sm-6 col-sm-offset-3" >
                            <form>
                                <div className="form-group" >
                                    <label>Email</label>
                                    <input type="text" className="form-control" />
                                </div>
                                <div className="form-group" >
                                    <label>Full Name</label>
                                    <input type="text" className="form-control" />
                                </div>
                                <div className="form-group" >
                                    <label>username</label>
                                    <input type="text" className="form-control" />
                                </div>
```

```
                    <div className="form-group" >
                        <label>Password</label>
                        <input type="password" className="form-control" />
                        </div>
                        <div className="form-group" >
                            <button className="btn btn-info" >Signup</button>
                        </div>
                    </form>
                </div>
            </div>
        </div>
    </div>
    );
  }
}
```

Login Component

```
class Login extends React.Component{
    render() {
        return (
            <div>
                <div className="container" >
                    <div className="row" >
```

```jsx
            <div className="col-sm-6 col-sm-offset-3" >
              <form>
                <div className="form-group" >
                  <label>username</label>
                  <input type="text" className="form-control" />
                </div>
                <div className="form-group" >
                  <label>Password</label>
                  <input type="password" className="form-control" />
                </div>
                <div className="form-group" >
                  <button className="btn btn-info" >Login</button>
                </div>
              </form>
            </div>
          </div>
        </div>
      </div>
    );
  }
}
```

Now we have prepared all our components, and we have used bootstrap classes, so don't forget to add bootstrap in index.js

```
<link rel="stylesheet" type="text/css" href="https://maxcdn.bootstrapcdn.com/bootstrap/3.3.7/css/bootstrap.min.css">
```

Now let's go to router.html#/signup, If everything compiled successfully, React will greet us with:

If you try to go to router.html#/contact, The app will greet you with:

It seems our router is working, from navigation you can try to visit different parts of applications. This is our whole React file:

```html
<!DOCTYPE html>
<html>
<head>
    <title>React Hello World</title>
    <link rel="stylesheet" type="text/css" href="https://maxcdn.bootstrapcdn.com/bootstrap/3.3.7/css/bootstrap.min.css">
</head>
<body>
    <div id="root" ></div>
    <script type="text/javascript" src="react.min.js" ></script>
    <script type="text/javascript" src="react-dom.min.js" ></script>
    <script type="text/javascript" src="react_router.js" ></script>
    <script type="text/javascript" src="browser.min.js" ></script>
    <script type="text/babel">
```

```
class Navbar extends React.Component{
    render() {
        return (
            <div className='navbar navbar-default' >
                <div className='container' >
                    <div className='navbar-header' >
                        <a className='navbar-brand' >React</a>
                    </div>
                    <div className='collapse navbar-collapse' >
                        <ul className='navbar-nav nav navbar-right' >
                            <li>
                                <a href="#/" >Home</a>
                            </li>
                            <li>
                                <a href="#/about" >About</a>
                            </li>
                            <li>
                                <a href="#/contact" >Contact</a>
                            </li>
                            <li>
                                <a href="#/login" >Login</a>
                            </li>
                            <li>
                                <a href="#/signup" >Signup</a>
                            </li>
                        </ul>
                    </div>
```

```jsx
          </div>
        </div>
      );
    }
  }


    class Home extends React.Component{
      render() {
        return (
          <div>
            <div className="container" >
              <div className="col-sm-6 col-sm-offset-3" >
                <h1>Welcome to our React App</h1>
                <p>
                  tempor incididunt ut labore et dolore magna aliqua. Ut enim ad minim veniam,
                </p>
              </div>
            </div>
          </div>
        );
      }
    }


    class About extends React.Component{
      render() {
        return (
```

```jsx
    <div>
      <div className="container" >
        <div className="row" >
          <div className="col-sm-6 col-sm-offset-3" >
            <h1>Welcome to about us page</h1>
            <p>
              Lorem ipsum dolor sit amet, consectetur adipisicing elit, sed do eiusmod
            </p>
          </div>
        </div>
      </div>
    </div>
  );
 }
}


class Contact extends React.Component{
  render() {
    return (
      <div>
        <div className="container" >
          <div className="row" >
            <div className="col-sm-6 col-sm-offset-3" >
              <form>
                <div className="form-group" >
                  <label>Name</label>
```

```jsx
                        <input className="form-control" placeholder="name" type="text" ></input>
                      </div>
                      <div className="form-group" >
                        <label>Email</label>
                        <input className="form-control" placeholder="name" type="text" ></input>
                      </div>
                      <div className="form-group" >
                        <label>Message</label>
                        <textarea className="form-control" placeholder="name" type="text" ></textarea>
                      </div>
                      <div className="form-group" >
                        <button className="btn btn-info" >Contact</button>
                      </div>
                    </form>
                  </div>
                </div>
              </div>
            </div>
    );
  }
}

class Signup extends React.Component{
```

```jsx
render() {
    return (
        <div>
            <div className="container" >
                <div className="row" >
                    <div className="col-sm-6 col-sm-offset-3" >
                        <form>
                            <div className="form-group" >
                                <label>Email</label>
                                <input type="text" className="form-control" />
                            </div>
                            <div className="form-group" >
                                <label>Full Name</label>
                                <input type="text" className="form-control" />
                            </div>
                            <div className="form-group" >
                                <label>username</label>
                                <input type="text" className="form-control" />
                            </div>
                            <div className="form-group" >
                                <label>Password</label>
                                <input type="password" className="form-control" />
                            </div>
```

```jsx
                        <div className="form-group" >
                            <button className="btn btn-info" >Signup</button>
                        </div>
                    </form>
                </div>
            </div>
        </div>
    </div>
            );
        }
    }


    class Login extends React.Component{
        render() {
            return (
                <div>
                    <div className="container" >
                        <div className="row" >
                            <div className="col-sm-6 col-sm-offset-3" >
                                <form>
                                    <div className="form-group" >
                                        <label>username</label>
                                        <input type="text" className="form-control" />
                                    </div>
                                    <div className="form-group" >
```

```
                    <label>Password</label>
                    <input type="password" className="form-control" />
                  </div>
                  <div className="form-group" >
                    <button className="btn btn-info" >Login</button>
                  </div>
                </form>
              </div>
            </div>
          </div>
        </div>
      );
    }
  }


    class App extends React.Component {
      render() {
        return (
          <div>
            <Navbar />
            <ReactRouter.Router history={ReactRouter.hashHistory}>
              <ReactRouter.Route path="/" component={Home}>
              </ReactRouter.Route>
```

```
            <ReactRouter.Route path="/login"
component={Login}>
            </ReactRouter.Route>

            <ReactRouter.Route path="/signup"
component={Signup}>
            </ReactRouter.Route>


            <ReactRouter.Route path="/contact"
component={Contact}>
            </ReactRouter.Route>


            <ReactRouter.Route path="/about"
component={About}>
            </ReactRouter.Route>

          </ReactRouter.Router>
        </div>
      );
    }
  }

    var destination = document.querySelector("#root");
```

```
ReactDOM.render(
    <div>
        <App></App>
    </div>,
    destination
);
</script>
</body>
</html>
```

Now think in terms of URL parameters like **user/1**, **user/2**, lets build a Routing system for users.

Create two Component:

1. Users – that show all users
2. User - that show selected user

Users.js will list all users and user.js will show only one user who is selected. Now add users and user to routes in app.js

import React from 'react';
import Home from './home.js';
import Login from './login.js';

```jsx
import Users from './users.js';
import User from './user.js';
import Signup from './signup.js';
import Navbar from './navbar.js';
import Contact from './contact.js';
import About from './about.js';

import {Switch, BrowserRouter, Route } from 'react-router-dom';

export default class App extends React.Component{
  render() {
    return (
      <div>
        <Navbar />
        <BrowserRouter>
          <Switch>
            <Route path="/home" component={Home} />
            <Route path="/about" component={About} />
            <Route path="/users" component={Users} />
            <Route path="/user/:id" component={User} />
            <Route path="/contact" component={Contact} />
            <Route path="/signup" component={Signup} />
            <Route path="/login" component={Login} />
          </Switch>
        </BrowserRouter>
      </div>
    );
```

    }
}

We have added users and user to our route, Now add content to your **user.js** and **users.js**

User Component

```
class Users extends React.Component{
    render() {
        return (
            <div className='container' >
                <ul>
                    <li><a href='#/user/1' >John</a></li>
                    <li><a href='#/user/2' >Doe</a></li>
                    <li><a href='#/user/3' >Micheal</a></li>
                </ul>
            </div>
        );
    }
}
```

User Component

```
class Users extends React.Component{
    render() {
```

```
    return (
      <div className='container' >
        <ul>
          <li><a href='#/user/1' >John</a></li>
          <li><a href='#/user/2' >Doe</a></li>
          <li><a href='#/user/3' >Micheal</a></li>
        </ul>
      </div>
    );
  }
}
```

Now go to navbar.js and add link to users,

```
<li>
  <a href="/users" >Users</a>
</li>
```

This will take us to users, Users will look like this:

If we click one of the users, react router will take us to user view page.

Now we have got a working routing example. And this is our final exercise:

```html
<!DOCTYPE html>
<html>
<head>
    <title>React Hello World</title>
    <link rel="stylesheet" type="text/css" href="https://maxcdn.bootstrapcdn.com/bootstrap/3.3.7/css/bootstrap.min.css">
</head>
<body>
    <div id="root" ></div>
    <script type="text/javascript" src="react.min.js" ></script>
    <script type="text/javascript" src="react-dom.min.js" ></script>
    <script type="text/javascript" src="react_router.js" ></script>
    <script type="text/javascript" src="browser.min.js" ></script>
    <script type="text/babel">

        class Navbar extends React.Component{
            render() {
```

```jsx
return (
  <div className='navbar navbar-default' >
    <div className='container'  >
      <div className='navbar-header' >
        <a className='navbar-brand' >React</a>
      </div>
      <div className='collapse navbar-collapse' >
        <ul className='navbar-nav nav navbar-right' >
          <li>
            <a href="#/" >Home</a>
          </li>
          <li>
            <a href="#/about" >About</a>
          </li>
          <li>
            <a href="#/contact" >Contact</a>
          </li>
          <li>
            <a href="#/users" >Users</a>
          </li>

          <li>
            <a href="#/login" >Login</a>
          </li>
          <li>
            <a href="#/signup" >Signup</a>
          </li>
```

```
          </ul>
        </div>
      </div>
    </div>
  );
 }
}

class Users extends React.Component{
  render() {
    return (
      <div className='container' >
        <ul>
          <li><a href='#/user/1' >John</a></li>
          <li><a href='#/user/2' >Doe</a></li>
          <li><a href='#/user/3' >Micheal</a></li>
        </ul>
      </div>
    );
  }
}

class User extends React.Component{
  render() {
    var users = [
      ["John"],
```

```jsx
      ["Doe"],
      ["Micheal"],
    ];
    return (
      <div className='container' >
        You are viewing user: {users[0]}
        <br />
        <a href='#/users' >Users</a>
      </div>
    );
  }
}


class Home extends React.Component{
  render() {
    return (
      <div>
        <div className="container" >
          <div className="col-sm-6 col-sm-offset-3" >
            <h1>Welcome to our React App</h1>
            <p>
              tempor incididunt ut labore et dolore magna aliqua. Ut enim ad minim veniam,
            </p>
          </div>
        </div>
      </div>
```

```jsx
      );
    }
}

class About extends React.Component{
    render() {
        return (
            <div>
                <div className="container" >
                    <div className="row" >
                        <div className="col-sm-6 col-sm-offset-3" >
                            <h1>Welcome to about us page</h1>
                            <p>
                                Lorem ipsum dolor sit amet, consectetur adipisicing elit, sed do eiusmod
                            </p>
                        </div>
                    </div>
                </div>
            </div>
        );
    }
}

class Contact extends React.Component{
    render() {
        return (
```

```
<div>
    <div className="container" >
        <div className="row" >
            <div className="col-sm-6 col-sm-offset-3" >
                <form>
                    <div className="form-group" >
                        <label>Name</label>
                        <input className="form-control" placeholder="name" type="text" ></input>
                    </div>
                    <div className="form-group" >
                        <label>Email</label>
                        <input className="form-control" placeholder="name" type="text" ></input>
                    </div>
                    <div className="form-group" >
                        <label>Message</label>
                        <textarea className="form-control" placeholder="name" type="text" ></textarea>
                    </div>
                    <div className="form-group" >
                        <button className="btn btn-info" >Contact</button>
                    </div>
                </form>
            </div>
        </div>
```

```jsx
          </div>
        </div>
      );
    }
  }

  class Signup extends React.Component{
    render() {
      return (
        <div>
          <div className="container" >
            <div className="row" >
              <div className="col-sm-6 col-sm-offset-3" >
                <form>
                  <div className="form-group" >
                    <label>Email</label>
                    <input type="text" className="form-control" />
                  </div>
                  <div className="form-group" >
                    <label>Full Name</label>
                    <input type="text" className="form-control" />
                  </div>
                  <div className="form-group" >
                    <label>username</label>
```

```jsx
                        <input type="text" className="form-control" />
                      </div>
                      <div className="form-group" >
                        <label>Password</label>
                        <input type="password" className="form-control" />
                      </div>
                      <div className="form-group" >
                        <button className="btn btn-info" >Signup</button>
                      </div>
                    </form>
                  </div>
                </div>
              </div>
            </div>
        );
      }
    }


    class Login extends React.Component{
      render() {
        return (
          <div>
            <div className="container" >
              <div className="row" >
```

```jsx
            <div className="col-sm-6 col-sm-offset-3" >
                <form>
                    <div className="form-group" >
                        <label>username</label>
                        <input type="text" className="form-control" />
                    </div>
                    <div className="form-group" >
                        <label>Password</label>
                        <input type="password" className="form-control" />
                    </div>
                    <div className="form-group" >
                        <button className="btn btn-info" >Login</button>
                    </div>
                </form>
            </div>
          </div>
        </div>
      </div>
    );
  }
}


class App extends React.Component {
    render() {
```

```
            return (
              <div>
                <Navbar />
                <ReactRouter.Router history={ReactRouter.hashHistory}>
                  <ReactRouter.Route path="/" component={Home}>
                  </ReactRouter.Route>

                  <ReactRouter.Route path="/login" component={Login}>
                  </ReactRouter.Route>

                  <ReactRouter.Route path="/signup" component={Signup}>
                  </ReactRouter.Route>


                  <ReactRouter.Route path="/contact" component={Contact}>
                  </ReactRouter.Route>


                  <ReactRouter.Route path="/about" component={About}>
                  </ReactRouter.Route>
```

```
                <ReactRouter.Route path="/users" component={Users}>
                </ReactRouter.Route>

                <ReactRouter.Route path="/user/:id" component={User}>
                </ReactRouter.Route>

            </ReactRouter.Router>
          </div>
        );
      }
    }


    var destination = document.querySelector("#root");

    ReactDOM.render(
      <div>
        <App></App>
      </div>,
      destination
    );
  </script>
</body>
</html>
```

Now go ahead and copy this file content and paste it in a html file and you will be greeted with working example of React Routing.

Now chapter has been ended and I have a quiz from you. I hope you have better understand what React Router is. Router redirects us to page when we clicked on a link. How can you make this routing using JS code? Did you know about it?

In case you didn't know, we can redirect by using link by:

import { Route } from 'react-router-dom'

const Button = () => (
 <Route render={({ history}) => (
  <button
   type='button'
   onClick={() => { history.push('/new-location') }}
  >
   Click Me!
  </button>
)} />
)

Chapter Conclusion:

So, we have learned following things:

- Introducing React
- Main principles of React
- Building your first react app
- Components in React
- Styling in React
- Creating complex components
- Use ReactJS components with another library
- Transferring properties
- Dealing with State
- Integrating React with Yii 2
- Going from Data to UI
- The component lifecycle
- Creating a single page app using react router

Now let's move to Setting up ReactJS development environment!

Chapter 14
Setting up ReactJS development environment In Node JS

In this chapter, we will learn how to setup a development environment in ReactJS In this chapter we will learn following things:

- Creating React App.
- Building Project.

React provided us a cli command called create-react-app, we need it to install it globally

npm install -g create-react-app

After create-react-app installs successfully go ahead and create a new project:

create-react-app my-app

Using comment create-react-app my-app, this command will create a new directory and install our react app. This command gives directory listing:

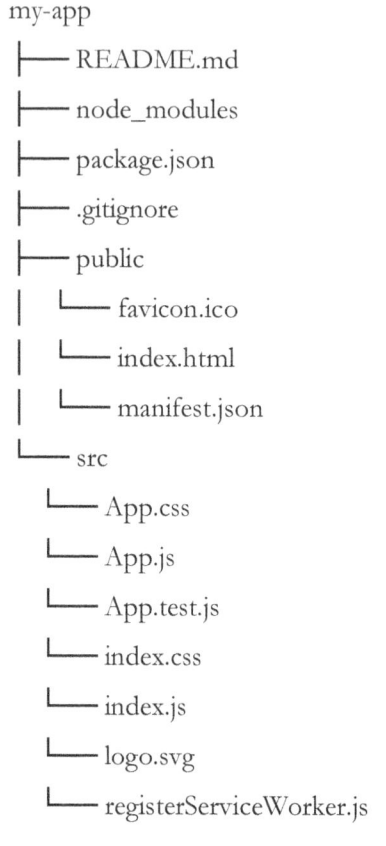

Folder Structure Explained:

- **Package.json**
  - This file contains info about installed modules
- **src/**
  - This folder contains source code.
- **public/**

○ This folder contains asset files for our app.
- **node_modules**
  ○ This folder contains all installed modules package.
- **.gitignore**
  ○ This file contains ignored files and folders for github push and pull.

After installation gets complete. Go to installed directory and run your app

cd my-app

You can use yarn or NPM to run ReactJS app:

npm start or yarn start

This command will initialize our app and if our application compiles successfully we will be greeted with React welcome screen:

We have setup a environment setup in our application. Now let's create our app build. We will need below command to build our app:

npm run build or yarn build

This will build our app in build folder. We will need to install serve globally to serve our build app. You can install serve globally by:

npm install -g serve

This will install serve globally and we can serve our application by:

serve -s build

This will run our build application on server:

http://localhost:5000

The same app will be run different server. But the application is ready to deploy!

As chapter has been ended and we have learned how to install Node JS based React JS. Here is a question for you:

How can you install this project with Yarn?

In case you didn't know how to install application with Yarn. Go ahead to https://yarnpkg.com/, and you can install yarn from here, you have follow following conditions to install Node JS using yarn:

yarn add create-react-app

This will install create-react-app and let us to initialize our Node JS based React Application.

Chapter Conclusion:

Now chapter has been ended and we have learned how to create Node JS based ReactJS application. Now let's move to chapter 15 where you will learn how to test Application with JEST.

Chapter 15
Test your React application with Jest

Did you ever hear about Jest? Jest is a testing platform. Facebook uses Jest to test all JavaScript code including their React applications. One of Jest's methods of insight is to give a coordinated "zero-configuration" understanding. We watched that when engineers are given prepared to-utilize instruments, they wind up composing more tests, which thusly brings about more steady and sound code bases.

Jest is a JavaScript tester maintained by Facebook Inc. Jest tester is a JavaScript software that looks for tests in codebase, runs them and displays the results (usually through a CLI interface).

Jest has following features:

- Easy Setup
- Instant Feedback
- Snapshot Testing for debugging

Fast and sandboxed

Jest parallelizes trials crosswise over specialists to expand execution. Console messages are cushioned and printed together with test comes about. Sandboxed test records and programmed worldwide state resets for each test so no two tests struggle with each other.

Built-in code coverage reports

Effortlessly make code scope reports utilizing - scope. No extra setup or libraries required! Joke can gather code scope data from whole undertakings, including untested records.

Zero configuration

Jest is as of now arranged when you utilize make respond application or respond local init to make your React and React Native activities. Place your tests in a __tests__ envelope, or name your test records with a .spec.js or .test.jsextension. Whatever you incline toward, Jest will discover and run your tests.

Works with TypeScript

Jest works with any arrange to-JavaScript dialect and coordinates consistently with Babel and with TypeScript through ts-jest.

Getting Started

Let's get started and install jest in our application and run a simple test, first we will need to install jest in our application:

By Npm:

```
npm install --save-dev jest
```

By Jest:

```
yarn add --dev jest
```

Both commands different but they install same jest in our react application.

Small Test

lets create a small test in our application, We can begin by composing a test for a theoretical capacity that includes two numbers. Create a file named sum.test.js under src/ directory. This will contain our actual test:

```
function sum(a, b) {
  return a + b;
}

test('adds 1 + 2 to equal 3', () => {
  expect(sum(1, 2)).toBe(3);
});
```

This will run a test to verify if a function returns 3 while adding numbers or by doing something else like **multiply, subtract** and **divide**. Go ahead and add this line to tests in package.json

```
"scripts": {
  "start": "react-scripts start",
  "build": "react-scripts build",
  "test": "jest",
  "eject": "react-scripts eject"
},
```

No go ahead and run npm t or npm test to run your test. If everything compiles successfully, your **CMD** should look like this.

```
C:\wamp\www\react\my-app>npm test

> my-app@0.1.0 test C:\wamp\www\react\my-app
> jest

 PASS  src\sum.test.js
   ✓ adds 1 + 2 to equal 3 (16ms)

Test Suites: 1 passed, 1 total
Tests:       1 passed, 1 total
Snapshots:   0 total
Time:        5.034s
Ran all test suites.

C:\wamp\www\react\my-app>
```

It means our app is successfully and our test is successfully passed. Now how to test React application with Jest, let's test our React application.

Testing Components

In this section, we will learn how to run test on React components. To run test on React components we need to install Jest with babel. Because we are using Babel we will install other modules that make Jest and Babel interact with each other:

npm install --save-dev babel-jest babel-polyfill babel-preset-es2015 babel-preset-react jest

This will install babel-jest, now create a file called .babelrc and put this content in it:

```
{
  "presets": ["es2015", "react"]
}
```

So, we can import other components in our test file and we can easily test other components. Now go ahead and create a file component.test.js that imports App component and run test:

import App from './app.js';

test('Checking component App', () => {

});

If everything runs fine, this code will test App component and as there are no errors in App component, So we will be greeted with PASS on CMD.

```
C:\wamp\www\react\my-app>npm t

> my-app@0.1.0 test C:\wamp\www\react\my-app
> jest

 PASS  src\component.test.js
  √ Checking component App (10ms)

Test Suites: 1 passed, 1 total
Tests:       1 passed, 1 total
Snapshots:   0 total
Time:        5.365s
Ran all test suites.

C:\wamp\www\react\my-app>
```

This means we have successfully tested our React Applications and it works fine and let's go ahead run ReactJS app with

npm start

This will start application server on http://localhost:3000, and we will greeted with app without errors.

Here is a quiz/question for you:

What actually JEST is?

In case you did not know what JEST is? Jest is delightful JavaScript testing. Jest has following features:

- Easy Setup.
- Instant Feedback.

- Snapshot testing.
- Zero Configuration Testing.
- Fast.
- Reports.
- Power mocking library.
- Works with typescript.

You can learn here more about JEST: https://facebook.github.io/jest/.

Chapter Conclusion

So now we have completed chapter 15 and we have learn how to install JEST and test your applications in it. Now go ahead to chapter 16 for Redux.

Chapter 16
Charge your React application with Redux

Do you have heard about Redux? Redux is a predictable state container for JavaScript apps.

It helps us to write applications that behave consistently, run in different environments (such as client, server, and native), and are easy to test. On top of that, it provides a great developer experience, such as live code editing combined with a time traveling debugger You can use Redux together with React, or with any other view library. Redux is very tiny (2kB, including dependencies).

Redux is created by Dan Abramov, Who works at Facebook. Redux is not for ReactJS, Redux is for the whole JavaScript. Redux is inspired by Facebook's Flux and influenced by functional programming language Elm.

Three Principles of Redux

There are 3 main principles of Redux, they are following

- **Single Source Of Truth**

The state of our whole application is stored in one object. Our whole application is depend on only one object. Which makes easier to understand and make changes to our states. We can call it single tree. A single state tree also makes it easier to debug or inspect an app.

console.log(store.getState())

```
/* Prints
{
  visibilityFilter: 'SHOW_ALL',
  todos: [
    {
      text: 'Consider using Redux',
      completed: true,
    },
    {
      text: 'Keep all state in a single tree',
      completed: false
    }
  ]
}
*/
```

- **State Is Read Only**

You cannot write state, meaning that you cannot mutate state directly. State is something we should read and pass it to ReactJS components. When we say, we cannot change state directly how do we change data inside our store? You do so by **actions** and **reducers** (will be explained shortly).

```
store.dispatch({
  type: 'COMPLETE_TODO',
  index: 1
})

store.dispatch({
  type: 'SET_VISIBILITY_FILTER',
  filter: 'SHOW_COMPLETED'
})
```

- **Changes are made with pure functions**

    Pure functions are those functions which returns expected result based on the parameters. They're purely synchronous not asynchronous. To make changes in our store we use these functions and we call them reducers. They don't mutate existing state rather they create a new state tree.

```js
function visibilityFilter(state = 'SHOW_ALL', action) {
  switch (action.type) {
    case 'SET_VISIBILITY_FILTER':
      return action.filter
    default:
      return state
  }
}

function todos(state = [], action) {
  switch (action.type) {
    case 'ADD_TODO':
      return [
        ...state,
        {
          text: action.text,
          completed: false
        }
      ]
    case 'COMPLETE_TODO':
      return state.map((todo, index) => {
        if (index === action.index) {
          return Object.assign({}, todo, {
            completed: true
          })
        }
        return todo
```

```
    })
  default:
    return state
 }
}

import { combineReducers, createStore } from 'redux'
const reducer = combineReducers({ visibilityFilter, todos })
const store = createStore(reducer)
```

This will Redux in our React application. Do you have ever think why we would need Redux in our application? Let's say we have a component called Main Component. And Main Component have child Components. If main component has to deliver states to its child components. They to make a relationship tree that will delivery states. But If there are lots of components and they have a lot of child components. What you should do? Store rescue us from this problem. That distributes states between components.

This is all about Redux! Now let's go ahead and install Redux in our React application.

We can install Redux by following command:

```
npm install redux --save
```

This will install Redux in our application.

Now go ahead into index.js

src/index.js

Import createStore from 'redux';

This will import createStore from Redux. Then we can create a new reducer also called functions:

```
const Reducer = (state, action) => {
        switch (action.type) {
                case 'ADD':
                        state = state + action.payload;
                        break;
                case 'SUBTRACT':
                        state = state - action.payload;
                        break;
        }
        return state;
}
```

That Adds and Subtracts numbers. Then we will create a new store.

```
const store = createStore(Reducer,0)
```

We created a store with initial value 0 for state to subtract and add. Then we can create a callback function that will run when a state is changed!

```
store.subscribe(() => {
        console.log("Store Updated!",store.getState());
});
```

Then we can dispatch the functions to add a number or to subtract a number.

```
store.dispatch({
        type: "ADD",
        payload: 3
});
store.dispatch({
        type: "ADD",
        payload: 1
});
```

Our final index.js file should Look alike:

```
import React from 'react';
import ReactDOM from 'react-dom';
import App from './app.js';
import 'bootstrap/dist/css/bootstrap.min.css';

import {createStore} from 'redux';
```

```
const Reducer = (state, action) => {
	switch (action.type) {
		case 'ADD':
			state = state + action.payload;
			break;
		case 'SUBTRACT':
			state = state - action.payload;
			break;
	}
	return state;
}
const store = createStore(Reducer,0);

store.subscribe(() => {
	console.log("Store Updated!",store.getState());
});

store.dispatch({
	type: "ADD",
	payload: 3
});
store.dispatch({
	type: "ADD",
	payload: 1
});
store.dispatch({
```

        type: "ADD",
        payload: 2
    });

ReactDOM.render(<App />,document.getElementById('root'));

Now go to your web console and see this will print on your console:

This means our Redux application is working! Right. so Create we can create another example, A working example. We will create a button click increment example. If a user clicks on a button, the counter will increment the times the button is clicked. let's create a folder called components and reducers under /src directory.

Now create below files with content:

src/components/Counter.js

import React, { Component } from 'react'
import PropTypes from 'prop-types'

export default class Counter extends Component {

```
constructor(props) {
  super(props);
  this.incrementAsync = this.incrementAsync.bind(this);
  this.incrementIfOdd = this.incrementIfOdd.bind(this);
}

incrementIfOdd() {
  if (this.props.value % 2 !== 0) {
    this.props.onIncrement()
  }
}

incrementAsync() {
  setTimeout(this.props.onIncrement, 1000)
}

render() {
  const { value, onIncrement, onDecrement } = this.props
  return (
    <p>
      Clicked: {value} times
      {' '}
      <button onClick={onIncrement}>
        +
      </button>
      {' '}
      <button onClick={onDecrement}>
```

          </button>
          {' '}
          <button onClick={this.incrementIfOdd}>
            Increment if odd
          </button>
          {' '}
          <button onClick={this.incrementAsync}>
            Increment async
          </button>
        </p>
)
    }
  }

Counter.propTypes = {
  value: PropTypes.number.isRequired,
  onIncrement: PropTypes.func.isRequired,
  onDecrement: PropTypes.func.isRequired
}

src/reducers/index.js

export default (state = 0, action) => {
  switch (action.type) {
    case 'INCREMENT':
      return state + 1

```
    case 'DECREMENT':
      return state - 1
    default:
      return state
  }
}
```

src/index.js

```
import React from 'react'
import ReactDOM from 'react-dom'
import { createStore } from 'redux'
import Counter from './components/Counter'
import counter from './reducers'

const store = createStore(counter)
const rootEl = document.getElementById('root')

const render = () => ReactDOM.render(
  <Counter
    value={store.getState()}
    onIncrement={() => store.dispatch({ type: 'INCREMENT' })}
    onDecrement={() => store.dispatch({ type: 'DECREMENT' })}
  />,
  rootEl
)
```

render()

store.subscribe(render)

This will give greet us with counter example:

Clicked: 11 times | + | - | Increment if odd | Increment async

Now go ahead try clicking the button to see the magic!

Here is quick quiz/question for you?

- Why do we use Redux?
- What is difference Between Redux and Flux?
- Who created Redux?

Why do we use Redux?

Redux gives a simple approach to concentrate the condition of your application. As a matter of first importance, Redux is difficult to at first handle. It has that kind of trouble bend that spikes straight up. The upside to this, in any case, is that after that underlying spike, you'll see that it drops off straightly. I never had such a variety of 'Ah-ha!' minutes taking in a structure as I did with Redux.

The quality behind Redux is React. Given an arrangement of designing information, React can easily change the obvious DOM starting with one state then onto the next. Redux expands upon this by being an anticipated state holder. That is, it gives sensible and unsurprising methods for keeping up your applications state in one place and making changes to it. When you match this with React, you get an application where you can look at your information, look at your perspectives, roll out one improvement to your information, and have a sensible doubt about how your perspectives will refresh.

What is difference between Redux and Flux?

In any case, to start with, I ought to likely bring up that Flux is an example and Redux is a library. Flux is a favor name for the eyewitness design altered a tiny bit to fit React.

Be that as it may, Facebook discharged a couple of devices to help in actualizing the Flux design, so the accompanying is the contrast between utilizing these devices (which is regularly alluded to as utilizing Flux) and utilizing Redux:

Both Flux and Redux have activities. Activities can be contrasted with occasions (or what trigger occasions). In Flux, an activity is a straightforward JavaScript question, and that is the default case in Redux as well, yet when utilizing Redux middleware, activities can likewise be capacities and guarantees.

With Flux it is a tradition to have numerous stores per application; each store is a singleton protest. In Redux, the tradition is to have a solitary store for every application, normally isolated into information spaces inside (you can make more than one Redux store if necessary for more mind boggling situations).

Flux has a solitary dispatcher and all activities need to go through that dispatcher. It's a singleton question. A Flux application can't have numerous dispatchers. This is required in light of the fact that a Flux application can have different stores and the conditions between those stores require a solitary chief, which is the dispatcher.

Redux has no dispatcher element. Rather, the store has the dispatching procedure heated in. A Redux store uncovered a couple of straightforward API capacities, one of them is to dispatch activities.

In Flux, the rationale of what to do on the information in view of the got activity is composed in the store itself. The store additionally has the adaptability of what parts of the information to uncover freely. The most brilliant player in a Flux application is the store.

In Redux, the rationale of what to do on the information in light of the got activities is in the reducer work that gets required each activity that gets dispatched (through the store API). A store can't be characterized without a reducer work. A Redux reducer is a straightforward capacity that gets the past state and one activity, and it restores the new state in view of that activity. In a Redux application, you can part your reducer into less difficult capacities as you would do with whatever other capacity. The most brilliant player in Redux is the reducer.

In Redux, likewise, there isn't a ton of adaptability about what to uncover as the store's state. Redux will simply uncover whatever came back from the store's reducer. This is one requirement.

The other greater requirement is that the store's state can't be variable (or truly, shouldn't be). There is no such limitation in Flux, you can change the state as you wish. The state's changelessness, in Redux, is accomplished effortlessly by making the reducers immaculate capacities (with no reactions). Reducers dependably duplicate the state they get and restores an altered variant of the state's duplicate, not simply the first question. While this is a major limitation, it makes life significantly less demanding long haul.

Who created Redux?

Redux is created by **Dan Abramov** around June 2015, he is software engineer at Facebook.

Chapter 17
Build And Go Beyond

So, we have learned:

- Main principles of React
- Building first react app
- Components in React
- Styling in React
- Creating complex components
- Use ReactJS components with another library
- Transferring properties
- Dealing with State
- Integrating React with Yii 2
- Going from Data to UI
- The component lifecycle
- React Router
- Setting up react development environment
- Testing React application with Jest
- Charging React application with Redux

We have learned how to build a react app and compiling it for production version. In this chapter, we will discuss about ReactJS Here are some questions that we will focus on this chapter:

- **Why you use React?**
- **Building Complex Components.**
- **Choosing Right Backend Framework in Rect.**
- **Choosing CSS libraries along with React**

Why you use React?

Here are some main reasons to learn react

1. **Fast Learning Curve:**

React is exceptionally a basic and lightweight library that lone manages the view layer. It is not a mammoth like other MV* structures, for example, Angular or Ember. Any JavaScript engineer can comprehend the essentials and begin building up an amazing web application after just several days perusing instructional exercise.

> As the React direct says 'Thinking in React' might be somewhat not quite the same as you used to since it conveys another way to deal with the table, yet it will turn out to be considerably less demanding and regular as you pick up involvement with it.

2. **Reusable Components:**

React gives a component based structure. Components are your Lego pieces. You begin with modest parts like a catch, check box, drop-down and so forth and you make wrapper segments made out of those littler segments. And afterward, you compose larger amount wrapper segments. Furthermore, it goes on like that until the point when you have this one root part and that segment is your application.

3. **Great Developer Tools**

Developer toolset is another essential factor when you are picking a development platform. There are two awesome tools you ought to know about: React Developer Tools and Redux Developer Tools. Both can be introduced as Chrome expansions.

4. **React Native**

Learning React accompanies a reward: React Native. React is not a 'compose once run anyplace library', as the makers say, it's a 'learn once compose anyplace' library. Yes, you can compose local applications for Android and IOS utilizing React Native. In spite of the fact that you won't have the capacity to utilize precisely the same you composed for web, you will have the capacity to utilize a similar philosophy and a similar engineering.

Building Complex Components:

As we discussed in chapter 6 to build complex components. Building complex is depend on your app idea. What type of idea you have? Is it a big idea? A big project? If your application is very big then you will need tons of components and sub components. Why? To split your web into components. To you can make changes to your web app. What type of idea you have? Is it a big idea? A big project? If your application is very big then you will need tons of components and sub components. Why? To split your web into components. To you can make changes to your web app. Let's suppose you have a large chat applications your component will be arranged like this:

```
<App>
    <AppNavbar>
        <AppNavbarBrand></AppNavbarBrand>

<AppNavbarBrandLinks></AppNavbarBrandLinks>
    </AppNavbar>
    <Grid padding='0' >
        <Half>
            <ChatSidebar></ChatSidebar>
        </Half>
        <Half>
            <ChatContent></ChatContent>
```

```
            </Half>
        </Grid>
        <Footer></Footer>
</App>
```

This is just imagination for chat application. It shows to how to create components. Again! Create a directory for these components:

- src/components/
  - /chat
    - ChatSidebar.js
    - ChatContent.js
- src/components/grid
  - Grid
  - Half
- Footer
  - Footer.js

Larger apps may have hundreds of components. This is very simplified component structure.

Choosing Right Backend Framework in React:

I would like to talk for PHP. What PHP application you want to use with your React? I recommend Laravel and/or Yii. Laravel is one of the most popular framework in PHP. Laravel is very fast framework and has huge community. Laravel is open source PHP framework, Laravel is very popular because it is easy to learn and open source. Currently, Laravel is supporting Vue JS. Laravel was launched on 2011, Laravel has successfully completed 6 years.

Yii is also great framework and it is a high-performance component-based PHP framework best for Web 2.0 development. Yii has frontend and backend support. I mean Yii gives us frontend website as well as admin panel for our website. Yii was originally launched on 2008.

Yii features include:

- Model View Controller Pattern
- Easy translation for different languages.
- Layered caching scheme, which supports data caching, page caching, and fragment caching and dynamic content. The storage medium of caching can be changed.
- Error handling and Error log caching.
- Best security features.
- Code generator for easy

Choosing CSS libraries along with React:

There are bunch of CSS frameworks and libraries you can use in your react app. Here are some popular CSS libraries you can use in React app:

- **Bootstrap**

Bootstrap, a sleek, intuitive, and powerful mobile first front-end framework for faster and easier web development. Bootstrap is written in SASS.

- **Bulma**

Bulma is an open source CSS framework based on Flex box and built with Sass. It's 100% responsive, fully modular, and available for free.

- **Semantic UI**

Semantic UI is probably one of most used CSS library of all time. Semantic UI is easy to implement in any project and we can easily embed plugin which we are using in our app. Semantic UI can be easily embed to React app. We can just simply use

npm install semantic-ui --save

to install Semantic UI in our application.

- **Foundation**

Foundation is a responsive front-end structure. Foundation gives a responsive framework and HTML and CSS UI parts, layouts, and code bits, including typography, shapes, catches, route and other interface components, and additionally discretionary usefulness given by JavaScript augmentations. Foundation Framework is kept up by ZURB and is an open source extend.

Conclusion

In this book we have learned about ReactJS React Components, React Router, How to run jQuery plugins in our React apps, Dealing with States, Building Complex components, Creating Single Page Apps using react router, Testing React with Jest, Charging our application with Redux.

Best of luck!

www.ingramcontent.com/pod-product-compliance
Lightning Source LLC
Chambersburg PA
CBHW050210230526
45470CB00001B/317